THE YALE SHAKESPEARE

EDITED BY

WILBUR L. CROSS   TUCKER BROOKE

PUBLISHED UNDER THE DIRECTION
OF THE
DEPARTMENT OF ENGLISH, YALE UNIVERSITY,
ON THE FUND
GIVEN TO THE YALE UNIVERSITY PRESS IN 1917
BY THE MEMBERS OF THE
KINGSLEY TRUST ASSOCIATION
TO COMMEMORATE THE SEVENTY-FIFTH ANNIVERSARY
OF THE FOUNDING OF THE SOCIETY

·: *The Yale Shakespeare* :·

THE SECOND PART OF KING HENRY THE SIXTH

EDITED BY

TUCKER BROOKE

LVX ET VERITAS

NEW HAVEN · YALE UNIVERSITY PRESS
LONDON · HUMPHREY MILFORD
OXFORD UNIVERSITY PRESS · MCMXXIII

TABLE OF CONTENTS

Copy 1

The facsimile opposite reproduces the title-page of the earliest version of the play later known as 'The Second Part of King Henry VI.' It is a good example of the descriptive title-page designed for advertising purposes. Only two or three copies are known, of which the one reproduced is in the Bodleian Library, Oxford.

THE
First part of the Con=

tention betwixt the two famous Houses of Yorke
and Lancaster, with the death of the good
Duke Humphrey:

And the banishment and death of the Duke of
Suffolke, and the Tragicall end of the proud Cardinall
of *VVinchester*, vvith the notable Rebellion
of *Iacke Cade:*

*And the Duke of Yorkes first claime vnto the
Crowne.*

LONDON

Printed by Thomas Creed, for Thomas Millington,
and are to be sold at his shop vnder Saint Peters
Church in Cornwall.
1594.

[DRAMATIS PERSONÆ

KING HENRY THE SIXTH
DUKE OF GLOUCESTER, *Uncle to the King*
CARDINAL BEAUFORT, *Great-Uncle to the King*
DUKE OF YORK
EDWARD }
RICHARD } *Sons of York*
DUKE OF SOMERSET
DUKE OF BUCKINGHAM
MARQUESS OF SUFFOLK
EARL OF SALISBURY
EARL OF WARWICK, *Son of Salisbury*
LORD CLIFFORD
YOUNG CLIFFORD, *his Son*
LORD SCALES, *Governor of the Tower*
LORD SAY
SIR JOHN STANLEY
SIR HUMPHREY STAFFORD
WILLIAM STAFFORD, *his Brother*
VAUX, *a Gentleman of the Court*
MATTHEW GOFFE, *a Captain under Lord Scales*
ALEXANDER IDEN, *a Gentleman of Kent*
Two Gentlemen, *Prisoners with Suffolk*
A Lieutenant of a Warship, Master, and Master's Mate
WALTER WHITMORE, *an Officer under the Lieutenant*
JACK CADE, *a Rebel Leader*
JOHN HUME }
JOHN SOUTHWELL } *Priests*
ROGER BOLINGBROKE, *a Scholar and Conjurer*
Mayor of Saint Albans
Clerk of Chatham
SIMPCOX, *an Impostor*
GEORGE BEVIS, JOHN HOLLAND, DICK the Butcher, SMITH the
    Weaver, MICHAEL, and other Followers of Cade
THOMAS HORNER, *an Armourer*
PETER THUMP, *his Apprentice*
Two Murderers
A Spirit raised by Bolingbroke

MARGARET OF ANJOU, *Queen to King Henry*
ELEANOR, *Duchess of Gloucester*
MARGERY JORDAN, *a Witch*
Simpcox's Wife
Lords, Ladies, and Attendants; Herald, Petitioners, Alder-
    men, a Beadle, Sheriff, and Officers; Citizens, Apprentices,
    Falconers, Soldiers, Messengers, etc.

SCENE: *London and its environs, Saint Albans, Bury St.
Edmunds, Kenilworth Castle, and several parts of Kent.*]

The Second Part of Henry the Sixth, with the Death of the Good Duke Humphrey

ACT FIRST

Scene One

[*London.   A Room of State in the Palace*]

Flourish of Trumpets: then hautboys.   Enter King,
*   Duke Humphrey, Salisbury, Warwick, and Beau-*
*   fort, on the one side.   The Queen, Suffolk, York,*
*   Somerset, and Buckingham on the other.*

Suf. As by your high imperial majesty
I had in charge at my depart for France,
As procurator to your excellence,
To marry Princess Margaret for your Grace;   4
So, in the famous ancient city, Tours,
In presence of the Kings of France and Sicil,
The Dukes of Orleans, Calaber, Britaine, and Alençon,
Seven earls, twelve barons, and twenty reverend
      bishops,   8
I have perform'd my task, and was espous'd:
And humbly now upon my bended knee,
In sight of England and her lordly peers,
Deliver up my title in the queen   12
To your most gracious hands, that are the substance
Of that great shadow I did represent;
The happiest gift that ever marquess gave,
The fairest queen that ever king receiv'd.   16

The Second . . . Henry the Sixth; *cf. n.*
2 had in charge: *was commissioned*   depart: *departure*
3 procurator: *proxy*
6 Sicil: *Réné, Margaret's father, titular king of Sicily*

King. Suffolk, arise. Welcome, Queen Margaret:
I can express no kinder sign of love
Than this kind kiss. O Lord, that lends me life,
Lend me a heart replete with thankfulness!   20
For thou hast given me in this beauteous face
A world of earthly blessings to my soul,
If sympathy of love unite our thoughts.

    Queen. Great King of England and my gracious
        lord,   24
The mutual conference that my mind hath had
By day, by night, waking, and in my dreams,
In courtly company, or at my beads,
With you, mine alderliefest sovereign,   28
Makes me the bolder to salute my king
With ruder terms, such as my wit affords,
And over-joy of heart doth minister.

    King. Her sight did ravish, but her grace in
        speech,   32
Her words yclad with wisdom's majesty,
Makes me from wondering fall to weeping joys;
Such is the fulness of my heart's content.
Lords, with one cheerful voice welcome my love.   36

    All kneel [*and say*]. Long live Queen Margaret,
        England's happiness!

    Queen. We thank you all.   *Flourish.*

    Suf. My Lord Protector, so it please your Grace,
Here are the articles of contracted peace   40
Between our sovereign and the French King Charles,
For eighteen months concluded by consent.

    Glo. Reads. 'Imprimis, It is agreed between the
French king, Charles, and William De la Pole, 44

18 kinder: *more natural*   25 mutual: *intimate*
27 beads: *prayers*   28 alderliefest: *dearest of all*
30 ruder: *too rude*   31 over-joy: *excessive joy*
33 yclad: *garbed*   43 Imprimis: *in the first place*

Marquess of Suffolk, ambassador for Henry
King of England, that the said Henry shall
espouse the Lady Margaret, daughter unto
Reignier King of Naples, Sicilia, and Jeru- 48
salem, and crown her Queen of England ere the
thirtieth of May next ensuing.

'Item, That the duchy of Anjou and the county
of Maine shall be released and delivered to the 52
king her father—'   [*Lets the paper fall.*]

King. Uncle, how now!

Glo.   Pardon me, gracious lord;
Some sudden qualm hath struck me at the heart
And dimm'd mine eyes, that I can read no further. 56

King. Uncle of Winchester, I pray, read on.

Win. 'Item, It is further agreed between
them, that the duchies of Anjou and Maine
shall be released and delivered over to the king 60
her father; and she sent over of the King of
England's own proper cost and charges, without having any dowry.'

King. They please us well. Lord Marquess, kneel
down: 64
We here create thee the first Duke of Suffolk,
And girt thee with the sword. Cousin of York,
We here discharge your Grace from being regent
I' the parts of France, till term of eighteen months 68
Be full expir'd. Thanks, uncle Winchester,
Gloucester, York, Buckingham, Somerset,
Salisbury, and Warwick;
We thank you all for this great favour done, 72
In entertainment to my princely queen.

---

51 Item: *likewise*
57 Uncle of Winchester: *Beaufort was the king's half-great-uncle*
58-63 *Cf. n.*
                              62 proper: *personal*
65 *Cf. n.*
                              66 girt: *gird*
68, 69 till . . . expir'd; *cf. n.*   73 entertainment: *service*

Come, let us in, and with all speed provide
To see her coronation be perform'd.

              Exit King, [with] Queen, and Suffolk.
                        Mane[n]t the rest.

    Glo. Brave peers of England, pillars of the state, 76
To you Duke Humphrey must unload his grief,
Your grief, the common grief of all the land.
What! did my brother Henry spend his youth,
His valour, coin, and people, in the wars?   80
Did he so often lodge in open field,
In winter's cold, and summer's parching heat,
To conquer France, his true inheritance?
And did my brother Bedford toil his wits,   84
To keep by policy what Henry got?
Have you yourselves, Somerset, Buckingham,
Brave York, Salisbury, and victorious Warwick,
Receiv'd deep scars in France and Normandy? 88
Or hath mine uncle Beaufort and myself,
With all the learned council of the realm,
Studied so long, sat in the council-house
Early and late, debating to and fro   92
How France and Frenchmen might be kept in awe?
And hath his highness in his infancy
Been crown'd in Paris, in despite of foes?
And shall these labours and these honours die? 96
Shall Henry's conquest, Bedford's vigilance,
Your deeds of war and all our counsel die?
O peers of England! shameful is this league,
Fatal this marriage, cancelling your fame,   100
Blotting your names from books of memory,
Razing the characters of your renown,
Defacing monuments of conquer'd France,

75 S. d. Manent: *remain on the stage*
79 my brother Henry: *Henry V*   85 policy: *administration*
101 books of memory: *chronicles of honor*
102 Razing the characters: *erasing the record*   103 Defacing: *effacing*

Undoing all, as all had never been.   104

   Car. Nephew, what means this passionate discourse,
This peroration with such circumstance?
For France, 'tis ours; and we will keep it still.

   Glo. Ay, uncle; we will keep it, if we can;   108
But now it is impossible we should.
Suffolk, the new-made duke that rules the roast,
Hath given the duchies of Anjou and Maine
Unto the poor King Reignier, whose large style   112
Agrees not with the leanness of his purse.

   Sal. Now, by the death of him who died for all,
These counties were the keys of Normandy.
But wherefore weeps Warwick, my valiant son?   116

   War. For grief that they are past recovery:
For, were there hope to conquer them again,
My sword should shed hot blood, mine eyes no tears.
Anjou and Maine! myself did win them both;   120
Those provinces these arms of mine did conquer:
And are the cities, that I got with wounds,
Deliver'd up again with peaceful words?
Mort Dieu!   124

   York. For Suffolk's duke, may he be suffocate,
That dims the honour of this warlike isle!
France should have torn and rent my very heart
Before I would have yielded to this league.   128
I never read but England's kings have had
Large sums of gold and dowries with their wives;
And our King Henry gives away his own,
To match with her that brings no vantages.   132

   Glo. A proper jest, and never heard before,
That Suffolk should demand a whole fifteenth

106 *This so detailed harangue*
112 large style: *inflated titles*
125 For: *as for; cf. n.*
134 fifteenth; *cf. n.*

110 rules the roast: *domineers*
120 *Cf. n.*
132 no vantages: *nothing but herself*

For costs and charges in transporting her!
She should have stay'd in France, and starv'd in
    France,   136
Before—

    Car. My Lord of Gloucester, now ye grow too hot:
It was the pleasure of my lord the king.

    Glo. My Lord of Winchester, I know your mind: 140
'Tis not my speeches that you do mislike,
But 'tis my presence that doth trouble ye.
Rancour will out: proud prelate, in thy face
I see thy fury. If I longer stay,   144
We shall begin our ancient bickerings.
Lordings, farewell; and say, when I am gone,
I prophesied France will be lost ere long.

                            Exit Humphrey.

    Car. So, there goes our protector in a rage. 148
'Tis known to you he is mine enemy,
Nay, more, an enemy unto you all,
And no great friend, I fear me, to the king.
Consider lords, he is the next of blood,   152
And heir apparent to the English crown:
Had Henry got an empire by his marriage,
And all the wealthy kingdoms of the west,
There's reason he should be displeas'd at it.   156
Look to it, lords; let not his smoothing words
Bewitch your hearts; be wise and circumspect.
What though the common people favour him,
Calling him, 'Humphrey, the good Duke of Glouces-
    ter;'   160
Clapping their hands, and crying with loud voice,
'Jesu maintain your royal excellence!'
With 'God preserve the good Duke Humphrey!'

145 our . . . bickerings; *cf. n.*   153 heir apparent; *cf. n.*
155 *Cf. n.*   157 smoothing: *ingratiating*

I fear me, lords, for all this flattering gloss, 164
He will be found a dangerous protector.

Buck. Why should he then protect our sovereign,
He being of age to govern of himself?
Cousin of Somerset, join you with me, 168
And all together, with the Duke of Suffolk,
We'll quickly hoise Duke Humphrey from his seat.

Car. This weighty business will not brook delay;
I'll to the Duke of Suffolk presently. 172

Exit Cardinal.

Som. Cousin of Buckingham, though Humphrey's
  pride
And greatness of his place be grief to us,
Yet let us watch the haughty cardinal:
His insolence is more intolerable 176
Than all the princes in the land beside:
If Gloucester be displac'd, he'll be protector.

Buck. Or thou, or I, Somerset, will be protector,
Despite Duke Humphrey or the cardinal. 180

Exit Buckingham, and Somerset.

Sal. Pride went before, ambition follows him.
While these do labour for their own preferment,
Behoves it us to labour for the realm.
I never saw but Humphrey, Duke of Gloucester, 184
Did bear him like a noble gentleman.
Oft have I seen the haughty cardinal
More like a soldier than a man o' the church,
As stout and proud as he were lord of all, 188
Swear like a ruffian and demean himself
Unlike the ruler of a commonweal.
Warwick, my son, the comfort of my age,
Thy deeds, thy plainness, and thy housekeeping 192

164 flattering gloss: *specious flattery*   167 of age; *cf. n.*
170 hoise: *hoist*   177 all: *that of all*   179 Or: *either*
181 Pride . . . ambition; *cf. n.*   188 as: *as if*
189 demean: *behave*   192 housekeeping: *hospitality*

Hath won the greatest favour of the commons,
Excepting none but good Duke Humphrey:
And, brother York, thy acts in Ireland,
In bringing them to civil discipline,   196
Thy late exploits done in the heart of France,
When thou wert regent for our sovereign,
Have made thee fear'd and honour'd of the people.
Join we together for the public good,   200
In what we can to bridle and suppress
The pride of Suffolk and the cardinal,
With Somerset's and Buckingham's ambition;
And, as we may, cherish Duke Humphrey's deeds, 204
While they do tend the profit of the land.

 War. So God help Warwick, as he loves the land,
And common profit of his country!

 York. And so says York, [*Aside.*] for he hath greatest cause.   208

 Sal. Then let's make haste away, and look unto the
  main.

 War. Unto the main! O father, Maine is lost!
That Maine which by main force Warwick did win,
And would have kept so long as breath did last.   212
Main chance, father, you meant; but I meant Maine,
Which I will win from France, or else be slain.

   Exit Warwick, and Salisbury. Manet York.

 York. Anjou and Maine are given to the French;
Paris is lost; the state of Normandy   216
Stands on a tickle point now they are gone.
Suffolk concluded on the articles,
The peers agreed, and Henry was well pleas'd
To change two dukedoms for a duke's fair daughter. 220

193 Hath; *cf. n.*
196 civil: *orderly*
209 main: *the most important thing at stake (from game of hazard)*
217 tickle: *slippery*
195 brother York; *cf. n.*
204 cherish: *foster, support*
218 concluded: *decided*

I cannot blame them all: what is 't to them?
'Tis thine they give away, and not their own.
Pirates may make cheap pennyworths of their pillage,
And purchase friends, and give to courtezans,   224
Still revelling like lords till all be gone;
While as the silly owner of the goods
Weeps over them, and wrings his hapless hands,
And shakes his head, and trembling stands aloof,   228
While all is shar'd and all is borne away,
Ready to starve and dare not touch his own:
So York must sit and fret and bite his tongue
While his own lands are bargain'd for and sold.   232
Methinks the realms of England, France, and Ireland
Bear that proportion to my flesh and blood
As did the fatal brand Althæa burnt
Unto the prince's heart of Calydon.   236
Anjou and Maine both given unto the French!
Cold news for me, for I had hope of France,
Even as I have of fertile England's soil.
A day will come when York shall claim his own;   240
And therefore I will take the Nevils' parts
And make a show of love to proud Duke Humphrey,
And, when I spy advantage, claim the crown,
For that's the golden mark I seek to hit.   244
Nor shall proud Lancaster usurp my right.
Nor hold the sceptre in his childish fist,
Nor wear the diadem upon his head,
Whose churchlike humours fit not for a crown.   248
Then, York, be still awhile, till time do serve:
Watch thou and wake when others be asleep,
To pry into the secrets of the state;

223 pennyworths: *bargains*   226 While as: *while*   silly: *helpless*
234 proportion: *relation*   235, 236 *Cf. n.*
236 prince's heart: *heart of the prince*
241 take the Nevils' parts; *cf. n.*
248 churchlike humours: *pietistic temperament*

Till Henry, surfeiting in joys of love,   252
With his new bride and England's dear-bought queen,
And Humphrey with the peers be fall'n at jars:
Then will I raise aloft the milk-white rose,
With whose sweet smell the air shall be perfum'd,   256
And in my standard bear the arms of York,
To grapple with the house of Lancaster;
And, force perforce, I'll make him yield the crown,
Whose bookish rule hath pull'd fair England down. 260

          Exit York.

Scene Two

*[The Same. A Room in the Duke of Gloucester's
House]*

Enter Duke Humphrey and his wife Eleanor.

Elea. Why droops my lord, like over-ripen'd corn
Hanging the head at Ceres' plenteous load?
Why doth the great Duke Humphrey knit his brows,
As frowning at the favours of the world?   4
Why are thine eyes fix'd to the sullen earth,
Gazing on that which seems to dim thy sight?
What seest thou there? King Henry's diadem,
Enchas'd with all the honours of the world?   8
If so, gaze on, and grovel on thy face,
Until thy head be circled with the same.
Put forth thy hand, reach at the glorious gold:
What! is 't too short? I'll lengthen it with mine;   12
And having both together heav'd it up,
We'll both together lift our heads to heaven,
And never more abase our sight so low

254 at jars: *into squabbles*
259 force perforce: *by violent compulsion*
1 corn: *wheat (or other cereal grain)*
8 Enchas'd: *adorned*

        9 grovel . . . face; *cf. n.*

As to vouchsafe one glance unto the ground. 16

Hum. O Nell, sweet Nell, if thou dost love thy lord,
Banish the canker of ambitious thoughts:
And may that thought, when I imagine ill
Against my king and nephew, virtuous Henry, 20
Be my last breathing in this mortal world!
My troublous dream this night doth make me sad.

Elea. What dream'd my lord? tell me, and I'll re-
quite it
With sweet rehearsal of my morning's dream. 24

Hum. Methought this staff, mine office-badge in
court,
Was broke in twain; by whom I have forgot,
But, as I think, it was by the cardinal;
And on the pieces of the broken wand 28
Were plac'd the heads of Edmund Duke of Somerset,
And William De la Pole, first Duke of Suffolk.
This was my dream: what it doth bode, God knows.

Elea. Tut! this was nothing but an argument 32
That he that breaks a stick of Gloucester's grove
Shall lose his head for his presumption.
But list to me, my Humphrey, my sweet duke:
Methought I sat in seat of majesty 36
In the cathedral church of Westminster,
And in that chair where kings and queens are crown'd;
Where Henry and Dame Margaret kneel'd to me,
And on my head did set the diadem. 40

Hum. Nay, Eleanor, then must I chide outright:
Presumptuous dame! ill-nurtur'd Eleanor!
Art thou not second woman in the realm,
And the protector's wife, belov'd of him? 44
Hast thou not worldly pleasure at command,

18 canker: *eating sore, ulcer*
25 office-badge: *mark of authority (as Protector)*
32 argument: *testimony, proof*
42 ill-nurtur'd: *ill-bred, rude*

38 that chair; *cf. n.*

Above the reach or compass of thy thought?
And wilt thou still be hammering treachery,
To tumble down thy husband and thyself   48
From top of honour to disgrace's feet?
Away from me, and let me hear no more.

 Elea. What, what, my lord! are you so choleric
With Eleanor, for telling but her dream?   52
Next time I'll keep my dreams unto myself,
And not be check'd.

 Hum. Nay, be not angry; I am pleas'd again.

Enter Messenger.

 Mess. My Lord Protector, 'tis his highness' pleasure
You do prepare to ride unto Saint Albans,   57
Whereas the king and queen do mean to hawk.

 Hum. I go.   Come, Nell, thou wilt ride with us?
      Exit Humphrey [with Messenger].

 Elea. Yes, my good lord, I'll follow presently.   60
Follow I must; I cannot go before,
While Gloucester bears this base and humble mind.
Were I a man, a duke, and next of blood,
I would remove these tedious stumbling-blocks   64
And smooth my way upon their headless necks;
And, being a woman, I will not be slack
To play my part in Fortune's pageant.
Where are you there?   Sir John! nay, fear not, man, 68
We are alone; here's none but thee and I.

Enter Hume.

 Hume. Jesus preserve your royal majesty!
 Elea. What sayst thou? majesty!   I am but Grace.

47 hammering: *meditating*
49 *From highest honor to lowest disgrace*
54 check'd: *rebuked*
68 Sir John; *cf. n.*
    61 go before: *i.e. occupy the highest place*
     71 but Grace; *cf. n.*

Hume. But, by the grace of God, and Hume's
    advice,   72
Your Grace's title shall be multiplied.
    Elea. What sayst thou, man? hast thou as yet con-
      ferr'd
With Margery Jordan, the cunning witch,
With Roger Bolingbroke, the conjurer?   76
And will they undertake to do me good?
    Hume. This they have promised, to show your high-
      ness
A spirit rais'd from depth of under ground,
That shall make answer to such questions   80
As by your Grace shall be propounded him.
    Elea. It is enough: I'll think upon the questions.
When from Saint Albans we do make return
We'll see these things effected to the full.   84
Here, Hume, take this reward; make merry, man,
With thy confederates in this weighty cause.

                       Exit Eleanor.

    Hume. Hume must make merry with the duchess'
      gold!
Marry, and shall. But how now, Sir John Hume!   88
Seal up your lips, and give no words but mum:
The business asketh silent secrecy.
Dame Eleanor gives gold to bring the witch:
Gold cannot come amiss, were she a devil.   92
Yet have I gold flies from another coast:
I dare not say from the rich cardinal
And from the great and new-made Duke of Suffolk;
Yet I do find it so: for, to be plain,   96
They, knowing Dame Eleanor's aspiring humour,
Have hired me to undermine the duchess
And buzz these conjurations in her brain.

88 Marry . . . shall: *indeed he shall*
93 flies: *which flies*   coast: *quarter*

They say, 'A crafty knave does need no broker;'　　100
Yet am I Suffolk and the cardinal's broker.
Hume, if you take not heed, you shall go near
To call them both a pair of crafty knaves.
Well, so it stands; and thus, I fear, at last　　104
Hume's knavery will be the duchess' wrack,
And her attainture will be Humphrey's fall.
Sort how it will I shall have gold for all.　　　*Exit.*

Scene Three

[The Same. A Room in the Palace]

*Enter three or four Petitioners, the Armourer's man
[Peter] being one.*

1. Pet. My masters, let's stand close: my
Lord Protector will come this way by and by,
and then we may deliver our supplications in
the quill.　　4

2. Pet. Marry, the Lord protect him, for
he's a good man! Jesu bless him!

Enter Suffolk and Queen.

1. Pet. Here a' comes, methinks, and the
queen with him. I'll be the first, sure.　　8

2. Pet. Come back, fool! this is the Duke
of Suffolk and not my Lord Protector.

Suf. How now, fellow! wouldst anything
with me?　　12

1. Pet. I pray, my lord, pardon me: I took
ye for my Lord Protector.

Queen. [*Glancing at the Superscriptions.*]

100 broker: *agent, go-between*
3, 4 in the quill: *in a body*

106 attainture: *conviction*

'To my Lord Protector!' Are your supplications 16
to his lordship? Let me see them: what is thine?

1. Pet. Mine is, an't please your Grace,
against John Goodman, my Lord Cardinal's
man, for keeping my house, and lands, my wife 20
and all, from me.

Suf. Thy wife too! that is some wrong indeed.
What's yours? What's here? 'Against the
Duke of Suffolk, for enclosing the commons of 24
Melford!' How now, sir knave!

2. Pet. Alas! sir, I am but a poor peti-
tioner of our whole township.

Peter. [*Presenting his petition.*] Against my 28
master, Thomas Horner, for saying that the
Duke of York was rightful heir to the crown.

Queen. What sayst thou? Did the Duke of
York say he was rightful heir to the crown? 32

Peter. That my master was? No, forsooth: my
master said that he was; and that the king was
an usurper.

Suf. Who is there? 36

Enter Servant.

Take this fellow in, and send for his master
with a pursuivant presently. We'll hear more
of your matter before the king.

Exit [Servant with Peter].

Queen. And as for you, that love to be protected 40
Under the wings of our protector's grace,
Begin your suits anew and sue to him.

Tears the supplication.

Away, base cullions! Suffolk, let them go.

18-22 *Cf. n.*　　　　　　24, 25 enclosing . . . Melford; *cf. n.*
38 pursuivant: *herald's messenger*　　43 cullions: *wretches*

All. Come, let's be gone.   44

                           Exeunt [Petitioners].

   Queen. My Lord of Suffolk, say, is this the guise,
Is this the fashion in the court of England?
Is this the government of Britain's isle,
And this the royalty of Albion's king?   48
What! shall King Henry be a pupil still
Under the surly Gloucester's governance?
Am I a queen in title and in style,
And must be made a subject to a duke?   52
I tell thee, Pole, when in the city Tours
Thou ran'st a-tilt in honour of my love,
And stol'st away the ladies' hearts of France,
I thought King Henry had resembled thee   56
In courage, courtship, and proportion:
But all his mind is bent to holiness,
To number Ave-Maries on his beads;
His champions are the prophets and apostles;   60
His weapons holy saws of sacred writ;
His study is his tilt-yard, and his loves
Are brazen images of canoniz'd saints.
I would the college of the cardinals   64
Would choose him pope, and carry him to Rome,
And set the triple crown upon his head:
That were a state fit for his holiness.

   Suf. Madam, be patient: as I was cause   68
Your highness came to England, so will I
In England work your Grace's full content.

   Queen. Beside the haught protector, have we Beau-
      fort
The imperious churchman, Somerset, Buckingham,   72
And grumbling York; and not the least of these

54 a-tilt: *in tournament*
57 courtship: *courtliness*   proportion: *figure*
63 canoniz'd; *cf. n.*
                             71 haught: *proud*

But can do more in England than the king.

 Suf. And he of these that can do most of all
Cannot do more in England than the Nevils: 76
Salisbury and Warwick are no simple peers.

 Queen. Not all these lords do vex me half so much
As that proud dame, the Lord Protector's wife:
She sweeps it through the court with troops of ladies, 80
More like an empress than Duke Humphrey's wife.
Strangers in court do take her for the queen:
She bears a duke's revenues on her back,
And in her heart she scorns our poverty.   84
Shall I not live to be aveng'd on her?
Contemptuous base-born callet as she is,
She vaunted 'mongst her minions t'other day
The very train of her worst wearing gown   88
Was better worth than all my father's lands,
Till Suffolk gave two dukedoms for his daughter.

 Suf. Madam, myself have lim'd a bush for her,
And plac'd a quire of such enticing birds   92
That she will light to listen to the lays,
And never mount to trouble you again.
So, let her rest: and, madam, list to me;
For I am bold to counsel you in this.   96
Although we fancy not the cardinal,
Yet must we join with him and with the lords
Till we have brought Duke Humphrey in disgrace.
As for the Duke of York, this late complaint   100
Will make but little for his benefit:
So, one by one, we'll weed them all at last,
And you yourself shall steer the happy helm.

Sound a Sennet.

76 the Nevils; *cf. n.*   86 callet: *lewd woman*
88 worst wearing: *most unfashionable*
89 better worth: *worth more*   91 lim'd a bush: *set a snare*
92 quire: *choir, chorus*   birds: *decoy birds*   97 fancy: *love*
103 S. d. Sennet: *trumpet call for march of processions*

Enter the King, Duke Humphrey, Cardinal, Bucking-
ham, York, [Somerset,] Salisbury, Warwick, an
the Duchess.

King. For my part, noble lords, I care not which; 10
Or Somerset or York, all's one to me.

York. If York have ill demean'd himself in France
Then let him be denay'd the regentship.

Som. If Somerset be unworthy of the place,   10
Let York be regent; I will yield to him.

War. Whether your Grace be worthy, yea or no,
Dispute not that: York is the worthier.

Car. Ambitious Warwick, let thy betters speak.   11

War. The cardinal's not my better in the field.

Buck. All in this presence are thy betters, Warwick

War. Warwick may live to be the best of all.

Sal. Peace, son! and show some reason, Bucking-
        ham,
                                                   11

Why Somerset should be preferr'd in this.

Queen. Because the king, forsooth, will have it so.

Hum. Madam, the king is old enough himself
To give his censure: these are no women's matters. 120

Queen. If he be old enough, what needs your Grace
To be protector of his excellence?

Hum. Madam, I am protector of the realm;
And at his pleasure will resign my place.   124

Suf. Resign it then and leave thine insolence.
Since thou wert king,—as who is king but thou?—
The commonwealth hath daily run to wrack;
The Dauphin hath prevail'd beyond the seas;   128
And all the peers and nobles of the realm
Have been as bondmen to thy sovereignty.

105 *Cf. n.*   107 denay'd: *refused*
122 protector; *cf. n.*   128 The Dauphin; *cf. n.*

Car. The commons hast thou rack'd; the clergy's
    bags
Are lank and lean with thy extortions.   132

Som. Thy sumptuous buildings and thy wife's attire
Have cost a mass of public treasury.

Buck. Thy cruelty in execution
Upon offenders hath exceeded law,   136
And left thee to the mercy of the law.

Queen. Thy sale of offices and towns in France,
If they were known, as the suspect is great,
Would make thee quickly hop without thy head.   140

       Exit Humphrey.   [*The Queen drops her fan.*]
Give me my fan: what, minion! can ye not?

         She gives the Duchess a box on the ear.
I cry you mercy, madam, was it you?

Duch. Was 't I? yea, I it was, proud Frenchwoman:
Could I come near your beauty with my nails,   144
I'd set my ten commandments in your face.

King. Sweet aunt, be quiet; 'twas against her will.

Duch. Against her will! Good king, look to 't in
    time;
She'll hamper thee and dandle thee like a baby: 148
Though in this place most master wear no breeches,
She shall not strike Dame Eleanor unreveng'd.

             Exit Eleanor.

Buck. Lord Cardinal, I will follow Eleanor,
And listen after Humphrey, how he proceeds: 152
She's tickled now; her fume needs no spurs,
She'll gallop far enough to her destruction.

            Exit Buckingham.

       Enter Humphrey.

---

133 sumptuous buildings; *cf. n.*   134 treasury: *treasure*
139 suspect: *suspicion*   142 cry you mercy: *beg your pardon*
145 my ten commandments: *marks of my ten fingers; cf. n.*
149 most master: *the most masterful spirit*
152 listen after: *seek news of*   153 fume: *passion*

Hum. Now, lords, my choler being over-blown
With walking once about the quadrangle,   15
I come to talk of commonwealth affairs.
As for your spiteful false objections,
Prove them, and I lie open to the law:
But God in mercy so deal with my soul   16
As I in duty love my king and country!
But to the matter that we have in hand.
I say, my sovereign, York is meetest man
To be your regent in the realm of France.   164

Suf. Before we make election, give me leave
To show some reason, of no little force,
That York is most unmeet of any man.

York. I'll tell thee, Suffolk, why I am unmeet: 168
First, for I cannot flatter thee in pride;
Next, if I be appointed for the place,
My Lord of Somerset will keep me here,
Without discharge, money, or furniture,   172
Till France be won into the Dauphin's hands.
Last time I danc'd attendance on his will
Till Paris was besieg'd, famish'd, and lost.

War. That can I witness; and a fouler fact   176
Did never traitor in the land commit.

Suf. Peace, headstrong Warwick!

War. Image of pride, why should I hold my peace?

Enter Armourer [Horner] and his Man [Peter].

Suf. Because here is a man accus'd of treason: 180
Pray God the Duke of York excuse himself!

York. Doth any one accuse York for a traitor?

King. What mean'st thou, Suffolk? tell me, what
    are these?

169 for: *because*
172 discharge: *formal license to proceed to France*   furniture:
    equipment
174 Last time; *cf. n.*   176 fact: *misdeed*

Suf. Please it your majesty, this is the man 184
That doth accuse his master of high treason.
His words were these: that Richard, Duke of York,
Was rightful heir unto the English crown,
And that your majesty was an usurper. 188
    King. Say, man, were these thy words?
    Arm. An 't shall please your majesty, I never
said nor thought any such matter: God is my
witness, I am falsely accused by the villain. 192
    Pet. By these ten bones, my lords, he did
speak them to me in the garret one night, as
we were scouring my Lord of York's armour.
    York. Base dunghill villain, and mechanical, 196
'll have thy head for this thy traitor's speech.
do beseech your royal majesty
Let him have all the rigour of the law.
    Arm. Alas! my lord, hang me if ever I spake 200
the words. My accuser is my prentice; and
when I did correct him for his fault the other
day, he did vow upon his knees he would be even
with me: I have good witness of this: therefore 204
I beseech your majesty, do not cast away an
honest man for a villain's accusation.
    King. Uncle, what shall we say to this in law?
    Hum. This doom, my lord, if I may judge. 208
Let Somerset be regent o'er the French,
Because in York this breeds suspicion;
And let these have a day appointed them
For single combat in convenient place, 212
For he hath witness of his servant's malice.
This is the law, and this Duke Humphrey's doom.
    [*King.* Then be it so. My Lord of Somerset,
We make your Grace lord regent o'er the French.] 216

93 bones: *fingers* 196 mechanical: *plebeian*
08 doom: *judgment* 210 in: *in regard to* 215, 216 *Cf. n.*

Som. I humbly thank your royal majesty.

Arm. And I accept the combat willingly.

   Pet. Alas! my lord, I cannot fight: for God's
sake, pity my case! the spite of man prevaileth 2:
against me. O Lord, have mercy upon me! I
shall never be able to fight a blow. O Lord, my
heart!

Hum. Sirrah, or you must fight, or else be hang'(

   King. Away with them to prison; and the day 22
of combat shall be the last of the next month.
Come, Somerset, we'll see thee sent away.

                                   Flourish. Exeun

Scene Four

[*The Same. The Duke of Gloucester's Garden*]

*Enter the Witch [Margery Jordan], the two Priest
   [Hume and Southwell], and Bolingbroke.*

   Hume. Come, my masters; the duchess, I
tell you, expects performance of your promises.

   Boling. Master Hume, we are therefore pro-
vided. Will her ladyship behold and hear our
exorcisms?

   Hume. Ay; what else? fear you not her
courage.

   Boling. I have heard her reported to be a
woman of an invincible spirit: but it shall be convenient, Master Hume, that you be by her aloft
while we be busy below; and so, I pray you,
go in God's name, and leave us.   *Exit Hume*
Mother Jordan, be you prostrate, and grovel 1
on the earth; John Southwell, read you; and
let us to our work.

10 aloft: *i.e. on the balcony of the stage*

Enter Eleanor aloft.

Elea. Well said, my masters, and welcome all.   16
o this gear the sooner the better.

Boling. Patience, good lady; wizards know their
    times:
eep night, dark night, the silent of the night,
he time of night when Troy was set on fire;   20
he time when screech-owls cry, and ban-dogs howl,
nd spirits walk, and ghosts break up their graves,
hat time best fits the work we have in hand.
Iadam, sit you, and fear not: whom we raise   24
'e will make fast within a hallow'd verge.

*Here do the ceremonies belonging, and make the
    circle; Bolingbroke or Southwell reads, Con-
    juro te, &c. It thunders and lightens terribly;
    then the Spirit riseth.*

Spir. Adsum.
Witch. Asmath!
y the eternal God, whose name and power   28
hou tremblest at, answer that I shall ask;
or till thou speak, thou shalt not pass from hence.

Spir. Ask what thou wilt. That I had said and
    done!

Boling. First, of the king: what shall of him
    become?   32

Spir. The Duke yet lives that Henry shall depose;
ut him outlive, and die a violent death.

As the Spirit speaks, Southwell writes the answers.]

Boling. What fates await the Duke of Suffolk?

Spir. By water shall he die and take his end.   36

Well said: *well done*	17 gear: *business*
silent: *silent part*	21 ban-dogs: *chained watch-dogs*
break up: *tear open*	
hallow'd verge: *magic circle*	S. d. belonging: *appropriate*
that: *what*	31 That: *would that* done: *had it over*

Boling. What shall befall the Duke of Somerset?
Spir. Let him shun castles:
Safer shall he be upon the sandy plains
Than where castles mounted stand.
Have done, for more I hardly can endure.
Boling. Descend to darkness and the burning lake
False fiend, avoid!

Thunder and lightning.   Exit Spir

Enter the Duke of York and the Duke of Buckingha
with their Guard, and break in.

York. Lay hands upon these traitors and the
     trash.
Beldam, I think we watch'd you at an inch.
What, madam! are you there? the king and commo
     weal
Are deeply indebted for this piece of pains:
My Lord Protector will, I doubt it not,
See you well guerdon'd for these good deserts.
Elea. Not half so bad as thine to England's king,
Injurious duke, that threatest where's no cause.
Buck. True, madam, none at all. What call y
     this?   [*Showing her the papers*
Away with them! let them be clapp'd up close
And kept asunder. You, madam, shall with us:
Stafford, take her to thee.—
We'll see your trinkets here all forthcoming.
All, away!   *Exit [Guard, with Duchess, etc.*
Yo.k. Lord Buckingham, methinks you watch'd h
     well:
A pretty plot, well chosen to build upon!
Now, pray, my lord, let's see the devil's writ.

45 Beldam: *hag*   watch'd: *caught in the act*   at an inch: *precise*
51 Injurious: *insulting*
53 clapp'd up close: *closely imprisoned*   39 *Cf.*

What have we here?　　　　　　　　　　　*Reads.*
'The duke yet lives that Henry shall depose;
But him outlive, and die a violent death.'
Why, this is just,　　　　　　　　　　　　64
'*Aio te, Æacida, Romanos vincere posse.*'
Well, to the rest:
'Tell me what fate awaits the Duke of Suffolk?
By water shall he die and take his end.　　68
What shall betide the Duke of Somerset?
Let him shun castles:
Safer shall he be upon the sandy plains
Than where castles mounted stand.'　　　72
Come, come, my lords; these oracles
Are hardly attain'd, and hardly understood.
The king is now in progress towards Saint Albans;
With him, the husband of this lovely lady:　76
Thither goes these news as fast as horse can carry
　　them,
A sorry breakfast for my Lord Protector.
　　Buck. Your Grace shall give me leave, my Lord of
　　　　York,
To be the post, in hope of his reward.　　80
　　York. At your pleasure, my good lord.
Who's within there, ho!

　　　　　Enter a Servingman.

Invite my Lords of Salisbury and Warwick
To sup with me to-morrow night.　Away!　84
　　　　　　　　　　　　　　　　Exeunt.

65 *Cf. n.*　　　74 hardly: *with difficulty*　　　77 goes; *cf. n.*

ACT SECOND

Scene One

[St. Albans]

*Enter the King, Queen, Protector, Cardinal, and
    Suffolk, with Falconers halloing.*

Queen. Believe me, lords, for flying at the brook,
I saw not better sport these seven years' day:
Yet, by your leave, the wind was very high,
And, ten to one, old Joan had not gone out.   4
  King. But what a point, my lord, your falcon made,
And what a pitch she flew above the rest!
To see how God in all his creatures works!
Yea, man and birds are fain of climbing high.   8
  Suf. No marvel, an it like your majesty,
My Lord Protector's hawks do tower so well;
They know their master loves to be aloft,
And bears his thoughts above his falcon's pitch.   12
  Glo. My lord, 'tis but a base ignoble mind
That mounts no higher than a bird can soar.
  Car. I thought as much; he would be above the
    clouds.
  Glo. Ay, my Lord Cardinal; how think you by
    that?   16
Were it not good your Grace could fly to heaven?
  King. The treasury of everlasting joy.
  Car. Thy heaven is on earth; thine eyes and thoughts
Beat on a crown, the treasure of thy heart;   20
Pernicious protector, dangerous peer,
That smooth'st it so with king and commonweal!

1 flying . . . brook: *hawking for waterfowl*   2 day: *space of time*
4 *Cf. n.*   5 point: *position from which to attack the prey*
6 pitch: *height*
                                                   10 tower: *soar*
20 Beat on: *keep aiming at*   22 smooth'st it: *insinuatest*

Glo. What! cardinal, is your priesthood grown
   peremptory?
Tantæne animis cœlestibus iræ?   24
Churchmen so hot? good uncle, hide such malice;
With such holiness can you do it?
   Suf. No malice, sir; no more than well becomes
So good a quarrel and so bad a peer.   28
   Glo. As who, my lord?
   Suf.   Why, as you, my lord,
An 't like your lordly lord-protectorship.
   Glo. Why, Suffolk, England knows thine insolence.
   Queen. And thy ambition, Gloucester.
   King.   I prithee, peace, 32
Good queen, and whet not on these furious peers;
For blessed are the peacemakers on earth.
   Car. Let me be blessed for the peace I make
Against this proud protector with my sword!   36
   Glo. [*Aside to the Cardinal.*] Faith, holy uncle,
   would 'twere come to that!
   Car. [*Aside to Gloucester.*] Marry, when thou
   dar'st.
   Glo. [*Aside to the Cardinal.*] Make up no factious
   numbers for the matter;
In thine own person answer thy abuse.   40
   Car. [*Aside to Gloucester.*] Ay, where thou dar'st
   not peep: and if thou dar'st,
This evening on the east side of the grove.
   King. How now, my lords!
   Car.   Believe me, cousin Gloucester,
Had not your man put up the fowl so suddenly,   44
We had had more sport. [*Aside to Gloucester.*] Come
   with thy two-hand sword.

24 *Cf. n.*   26 *Cf. n.*
39 *Do not refer the quarrel to your followers*

Glo. True, uncle.

Car. Are ye advis'd? [*Aside to Gloucester.*] The east side of the grove.

Glo. [*Aside to the Cardinal.*] Cardinal, I am with you. 48

King. Why, how now, uncle Gloucester!

Glo. Talking of hawking; nothing else, my lord.— [*Aside to the Cardinal.*] Now, by God's mother, priest, I'll shave your crown

For this, or all my fence shall fail. 52

Car. [*Aside to Gloucester.*] *Medice, teipsum;* Protector, see to 't well, protect yourself.

King. The winds grow high; so do your stomachs, lords.

How irksome is this music to my heart! 56

When such strings jar, what hope of harmony?

I pray, my lords, let me compound this strife.

Enter one crying, 'A Miracle.'

Glo. What means this noise?

Fellow, what miracle dost thou proclaim? 60

One. A miracle! a miracle!

Suf. Come to the king, and tell him what miracle.

One. Forsooth, a blind man at Saint Alban's shrine,

Within this half hour hath receiv'd his sight; 64

A man that ne'er saw in his life before.

King. Now, God be prais'd, that to believing souls

Gives light in darkness, comfort in despair!

Enter the Mayor of Saint Albans, and his Brethren, bearing the man [Simpcox] between two in a chair [followed by Simpcox's wife and others].

46-48 *Cf. n.*　　　　　　　　　　　　　47 advis'd: *clearly informed*
52 fence: *skill in fencing*
53 Medice, teipsum: *Doctor, cure thyself*
55 stomachs: *angers*　　　　　　　　　　　57 jar: *sound a discord*
58 compound: *settle, compose*　　　　63 Saint Alban's shrine; *cf. n.*

Car. Here comes the townsmen on procession,   68
To present your highness with the man.

King. Great is his comfort in this earthly vale,
Although by his sight his sin be multiplied.

Glo. Stand by, my masters; bring him near the
    king: 72
His highness' pleasure is to talk with him.

King. Good fellow, tell us here the circumstance,
That we for thee may glorify the Lord.
What! hast thou been long blind, and now restor'd? 76

Simp. Born blind, an 't please your Grace.

Wife. Ay, indeed, was he.

Suf. What woman is this?

Wife. His wife, an 't like your worship.   80

Glo. Hadst thou been his mother, thou couldst have
    better told.

King. Where wert thou born?

Simp. At Berwick in the north, an 't like your Grace.

King. Poor soul! God's goodness hath been great
    to thee: 84
Let never day nor night unhallow'd pass,
But still remember what the Lord hath done.

Queen. Tell me, good fellow, cam'st thou here by
    chance,
Or of devotion, to this holy shrine?   88

Simp. God knows, of pure devotion; being call'd
A hundred times and oft'ner in my sleep,
By good Saint Alban; who said, 'Simon, come;
Come, offer at my shrine, and I will help thee.'   92

Wife. Most true, forsooth; and many time and oft
Myself have heard a voice to call him so.

Car. What! art thou lame?

Simp.   Ay, God Almighty help me!

71 *Although the recovery of his eyesight expose him to additional
temptations.*   74 circumstance: *details*   91 Simon; *cf. n.*

Suf. How cam'st thou so?

Simp.   A fall off of a tree. 96

Wife. A plum-tree, master.

Glo.   How long hast thou been blind?

Simp. O! born so, master.

Glo.   What! and wouldst climb a tree?

Simp. But that in all my life, when I was a youth.

Wife. Too true; and bought his climbing very
    dear.   100

Glo. Mass, thou lov'dst plums well, that wouldst
    venture so.

Simp. Alas! master, my wife desir'd some damsons,
And made me climb with danger of my life.

Glo. A subtle knave! but yet it shall not serve.   104
Let me see thine eyes: wink now: now open them:
In my opinion yet thou seest not well.

Simp. Yes, master, clear as day; I thank God and
    Saint Albans.

Glo. Sayst thou me so? What colour is this cloak
    of?   108

Simp. Red, master; red as blood.

Glo. Why, that's well said. What colour is my gown
    of?

Simp. Black, forsooth; coal-black, as jet.

King. Why then, thou know'st what colour jet is
    of?   112

Suf. And yet, I think, jet did he never see.

Glo. But cloaks and gowns before this day a many.

Wife. Never, before this day, in all his life.

Glo. Tell me, sirrah, what's my name?   116

Simp. Alas! master, I know not.

Glo. What's his name?

99 But that: *only that one tree*
104 serve: *serve his purpose, succeed*   105 wink: *close both eyes*
107 Saint Albans: *i.e. the saint's shrine*
                                                 114 many: *multitude*

Simp. I know not.

Glo. Nor his?   120

Simp. No, indeed, master.

Glo. What's thine own name?

Simp. Saunder Simpcox, an if it please you, master.

Glo. Then, Saunder, sit there, the lying'st 124
knave in Christendom. If thou hadst been born
blind, thou mightst as well have known all our
names as thus to name the several colours we do
wear. Sight may distinguish of colours, but 128
suddenly to nominate them all, it is impossible.
My lords, Saint Alban here hath done a miracle;
and would ye not think that cunning to be great,
that could restore this cripple to his legs again? 132

Simp. O, master, that you could!

Glo. My masters of St. Albans, have you
not beadles in your town, and things called
whips?   136

May. Yes, my lord, if it please your Grace.

Glo. Then send for one presently.

May. Sirrah, go fetch the beadle hither straight.

                              Exit [an Attendant].

Glo. Now fetch me a stool hither by and by. 140
[*A stool brought out.*] Now, sirrah, if you mean
to save yourself from whipping, leap me over
this stool and run away.

Simp. Alas! master, I am not able to stand alone: 144
You go about to torture me in vain.

                Enter a Beadle with whips.

Glo. Well, sir, we must have you find your
legs. Sirrah beadle, whip him till he leap over
that same stool.   148

129 nominate: *call by name*   140 by and by: *at once*
142 leap me: *leap*

Bead. I will, my lord. Come on, sirrah; off with your doublet quickly.

Simp. Alas! master, what shall I do? I am not able to stand. 152

After the Beadle hath hit him once, he leaps over the stool, and runs away: and they follow and cry, 'A miracle!'

King. O God! seest thou this, and bear'st so long?

Queen. It made me laugh to see the villain run.

Glo. Follow the knave; and take this drab away.

Wife. Alas! sir, we did it for pure need. 156

Glo. Let them be whipp'd through every market town

Till they come to Berwick, from whence they came.

Exit [Mayor, with Beadle, Wife, &c].

Car. Duke Humphrey has done a miracle to-day.

Suf. True; made the lame to leap and fly away. 160

Glo. But you have done more miracles than I;

You made in a day, my lord, whole towns to fly.

Enter Buckingham.

King. What tidings with our cousin Buckingham?

Buck. Such as my heart doth tremble to unfold. 164

A sort of naughty persons, lewdly bent,

Under the countenance and confederacy

Of Lady Eleanor, the protector's wife,

The ringleader and head of all this rout, 168

Have practis'd dangerously against your state,

Dealing with witches and with conjurers:

Whom we have apprehended in the fact,

Raising up wicked spirits from under ground, 172

Demanding of King Henry's life and death,

165 sort: *set*   naughty: *good-for-naught*   lewdly bent: *with evil intent*   168 rout: *company*   169 practis'd: *plotted*
171 in the fact: *red-handed*   173 Demanding of: *inquiring about*

And other of your highness' privy council,
As more at large your Grace shall understand.

  Car. And so, my Lord Protector, by this means 176
Your lady is forthcoming yet at London.
This news, I think, hath turn'd your weapon's edge;
'Tis like, my lord, you will not keep your hour.

  Glo. Ambitious churchman, leave to afflict my
    heart: 180
Sorrow and grief have vanquish'd all my powers;
And, vanquish'd as I am, I yield to thee,
Or to the meanest groom.

  King. O God! what mischiefs work the wicked
    ones, 184
Heaping confusion on their own heads thereby.

  Queen. Gloucester, see here the tainture of thy nest;
And look thyself be faultless, thou wert best.

  Glo. Madam, for myself, to heaven I do appeal, 188
How I have lov'd my king and commonweal;
And, for my wife, I know not how it stands.
Sorry I am to hear what I have heard:
Noble she is, but if she have forgot 192
Honour and virtue, and convers'd with such
As, like to pitch, defile nobility,
I banish her my bed and company,
And give her, as a prey, to law and shame, 196
That hath dishonour'd Gloucester's honest name.

  King. Well, for this night we will repose us here:
To-morrow toward London back again,
To look into this business thoroughly, 200
And call these foul offenders to their answers;
And poise the cause in justice' equal scales,

177 forthcoming: *under arrest*   180 leave: *cease*
180 leave: *cease*   187 thou wert best: *you had better*
186 tainture: *fouling*   202 poise: *weigh*
193 convers'd: *had dealings*

Whose beam stands sure, whose rightful cause pre-
　　vails.　　　　　　　　　　　　　　*Flourish.　Exeunt.*

Scene Two

[London.　The Duke of York's Garden]

Enter York, Salisbury, and Warwick.

York. Now, my good Lords of Salisbury and War-
　　wick,
Our simple supper ended, give me leave,
In this close walk to satisfy myself,
In craving your opinion of my title,　　　　　　　　　　4
Which is infallible to England's crown.
　　Sal. My lord, I long to hear it at full.
　　War. Sweet York, begin; and if thy claim be good,
The Nevils are thy subjects to command.　　　　　　　8
　　York. Then thus:
Edward the Third, my lords, had seven sons:
The first, Edward the Black Prince, Prince of Wales;
The second, William of Hatfield; and the third,　　　12
Lionel, Duke of Clarence; next to whom
Was John of Gaunt, the Duke of Lancaster;
The fifth was Edmund Langley, Duke of York;
The sixth was Thomas of Woodstock, Duke of
　　Gloucester;　　　　　　　　　　　　　　　　　16
William of Windsor was the seventh and last.
Edward the Black Prince died before his father,
And left behind him Richard, his only son,
Who after Edward the Third's death, reign'd as
　　king;　　　　　　　　　　　　　　　　　　　20
Till Henry Bolingbroke, Duke of Lancaster,
The eldest son and heir of John of Gaunt,

---

203 beam: *transverse balancing rod of scales*　　　3 close: *private*

Crown'd by the name of Henry the Fourth,
Seiz'd on the realm, depos'd the rightful king,   24
Sent his poor queen to France, from whence she came,
And him to Pomfret; where as all you know,
Harmless Richard was murther'd traitorously.

War. Father, the duke hath told the truth;   28
Thus got the house of Lancaster the crown.

York. Which now they hold by force and not by
     right;
For Richard, the first son's heir, being dead,
The issue of the next son should have reign'd.   32

Sal. But William of Hatfield died without an heir.

York. The third son, Duke of Clarence, from whose
     line
I claim the crown, had issue, Philippe a daughter,
Who married Edmund Mortimer, Earl of March: 36
Edmund had issue Roger, Earl of March:
Roger had issue Edmund, Anne, and Eleanor.

Sal. This Edmund, in the reign of Bolingbroke,
As I have read, laid claim unto the crown;   40
And but for Owen Glendower, had been king,
Who kept him in captivity till he died.
But, to the rest.

York.   His eldest sister, Anne,
My mother, being heir unto the crown,   44
Married Richard, Earl of Cambridge, who was son
To Edmund Langley, Edward the Third's fifth son.
By her I claim the kingdom: she was heir
To Roger, Earl of March; who was the son   48
Of Edmund Mortimer, who married Philippe,
Sole daughter unto Lionel, Duke of Clarence:
So, if the issue of the eldest son
Succeed before the younger, I am king.   52

39-42 This Edmund . . . died; *cf. n.*

War. What plain proceeding is more plain than this?
Henry doth claim the crown from John of Gaunt,
The fourth son; York claims it from the third.
Till Lionel's issue fails, his should not reign: 56
It fails not yet, but flourishes in thee,
And in thy sons, fair slips of such a stock.
Then, father Salisbury, kneel we together,
And in this private plot be we the first   60
That shall salute our rightful sovereign
With honour of his birthright to the crown.

   Both. Long live our sovereign Richard, England's
    king!

   York. We thank you, lords! But I am not your
    king   64
Till I be crown'd, and that my sword be stain'd
With heart-blood of the house of Lancaster;
And that's not suddenly to be perform'd,
But with advice and silent secrecy.   68
Do you as I do in these dangerous days,
Wink at the Duke of Suffolk's insolence,
At Beaufort's pride, at Somerset's ambition,
At Buckingham and all the crew of them,   72
Till they have snar'd the shepherd of the flock,
That virtuous prince, the good Duke Humphrey:
'Tis that they seek; and they, in seeking that
Shall find their deaths, if York can prophesy.   76

   Sal. My lord, break we off; we know your mind at
    full.

   War. My heart assures me that the Earl of Warwick
Shall one day make the Duke of York a king.

   York. And, Nevil, this I do assure myself,   80
Richard shall live to make the Earl of Warwick
The greatest man in England but the king.   *Exeunt.*

62 With . . . birthright: *acclaiming his hereditary right*

Scene Three

[*The Same. A Hall of Justice*]

*Sound Trumpets. Enter the King and State [includ-
ing Queen, Gloucester, York, Suffolk, and Salis-
bury], with Guard, to banish the Duchess. [Mar-
gery Jordan, Hume, Southwell, and Bolingbroke are
also brought in.]*

   King. Stand forth, Dame Eleanor Cobham, Glouces-
     ter's wife.
In sight of God and us your guilt is great:
Receive the sentence of the law for sins
Such as by God's book are adjudg'd to death.   4
You four, from hence to prison back again;
From thence, unto the place of execution:
The witch in Smithfield shall be burnt to ashes,
And you three shall be strangled on the gallows.   8
You, madam, for you are more nobly born,
Despoiled of your honour in your life,
Shall, after three days' open penance done,
Live in your country here in banishment,   12
With Sir John Stanley, in the Isle of Man.
   Elea. Welcome is banishment; welcome were my
     death.
   Glo. Eleanor, the law, thou seest, hath judged thee:
I cannot justify whom the law condemns.   16
                   [*Exeunt the Duchess, and the other
                         Prisoners, guarded.*]
Mine eyes are full of tears, my heart of grief.
Ah, Humphrey! this dishonour in thine age
Will bring thy head with sorrow to the ground.
I beseech your majesty, give me leave to go;   20
Sorrow would solace and mine age would ease.

4 *Cf. n.*   7, 8 *Cf. n.*   13 *Cf. n.*   21 would: *needs to have*

King. Stay, Humphrey, Duke of Gloucester: ere
    thou go,
Give up thy staff: Henry will to himself
Protector be; and God shall be my hope,   24
My stay, my guide, and lantern to my feet.
And go in peace, Humphrey; no less belov'd
Than when thou wert protector to thy king.

    Queen. I see no reason why a king of years   28
Should be to be protected like a child.
God and King Henry govern England's realm!
Give up your staff, sir, and the king his realm.

    Glo. My staff! here, noble Henry, is my staff: 32
As willingly do I the same resign
As e'er thy father Henry made it mine;
And even as willingly at thy feet I leave it
As others would ambitiously receive it.   36
Farewell, good king! when I am dead and gone,
May honourable peace attend thy throne.

                         Exit Gloucester.
    Queen. Why, now is Henry king, and Margaret
    queen;
And Humphrey, Duke of Gloucester, scarce himself, 40
That bears so shrewd a maim: two pulls at once;
His lady banish'd, and a limb lopp'd off,
This staff of honour raught: there let it stand,
Where it best fits to be, in Henry's hand.   44

    Suf. Thus droops this lofty pine and hangs his
    sprays;
Thus Eleanor's pride dies in her youngest days.

    York. Lords, let him go. Please it your majesty
This is the day appointed for the combat;   48
And ready are the appellant and defendant,

23 staff: *badge of office*   29 be to be: *need to be*
41 so . . . maim: *so sore a mutilation*   pulls: *pluckings of*
    feathers (?)*   43 raught: *seized*
46 youngest: *latest, most recent (?); cf. n.*   49 appellant: *challenger*

The armourer and his man, to enter the lists,
So please your highness to behold the fight.

   Queen. Ay, good my lord; for purposely there-
     fore   52
Left I the court, to see this quarrel tried.

   King. O' God's name, see the lists and all things fit:
Here let them end it; and God defend the right!

   York. I never saw a fellow worse bested,   56
Or more afraid to fight, than is the appellant,
The servant of this armourer, my lords.

Enter at one door the Armourer [Horner] and his
Neighbours, drinking to him so much that he is
drunk; and he enters with a drum before him, and
his staff with a sand-bag fastened to it: and at the
other door his Man [Peter], with a drum and sand-
bag, and Prentices drinking to him.

   1. Neigh. Here, neighbour Horner, I drink
to you in a cup of sack: and fear not, neigh- 60
bour, you shall do well enough.

   2. Neigh. And here, neighbour, here's a
cup of charneco.

   3. Neigh. And here's a pot of good 64
double beer, neighbour: drink, and fear not
your man.

   Arm. Let it come, i' faith, and I'll pledge you
all; and a fig for Peter!   68

   1. Pren. Here, Peter, I drink to thee; and
be not afraid.

   2. Pren. Be merry, Peter, and fear not thy
master: fight for credit of the prentices.   72

   Peter. I thank you all: drink, and pray for
me, I pray you; for, I think, I have taken my

54 O': *in*   56 bested: *prepared*
60 sack: *dry Spanish wine*   63 charneco: *sweet Portuguese wine*

last draught in this world. Here, Robin, an if I
die, I give thee my apron: and, Will, thou shalt 76
have my hammer: and here, Tom, take all the
money that I have. O Lord bless me! I pray
God, for I am never able to deal with my master,
he hath learnt so much fence already.　　　　　　80

Sal. Come, leave your drinking and fall to
blows. Sirrah, what's thy name?

Peter. Peter, forsooth.

Sal. Peter! what more?　　　　　　　　　　84

Peter. Thump.

Sal. Thump! then see thou thump thy master well.

Arm. Masters, I am come hither, as it were, 88
upon my man's instigation, to prove him a
knave, and myself an honest man: and touch-
ing the Duke of York, I will take my death I
never meant him any ill, nor the king, nor the 92
queen; and therefore, Peter, have at thee with
a downright blow!

York. Dispatch: this knave's tongue begins to
double.

Sound, trumpets, alarum to the combatants.　　96

　　　　　They fight, and Peter strikes him down.

Arm. Hold, Peter, hold! I confess, I confess
treason.　　　　　　　　　　　　　　*[Dies.]*

York. Take away his weapon. Fellow, thank
God, and the good wine in thy master's way.　100

Peter. O God! have I overcome mine enemies
in this presence? O Peter! thou hast prevailed
in right!

King. Go, take hence that traitor from our sight; 104
For by his death we do perceive his guilt:

---

91 take my death: *pledge my life* 　　　　　95 double: *talk thickly*
97, 98 I confess treason; *cf. n.*

And God in justice hath reveal'd to us
The truth and innocence of this poor fellow,
Which he had thought to have murther'd wrong-
    fully.   108
Come, fellow, follow us for thy reward.
                 Sound a flourish. Exeunt.

Scene Four

[*The Same. A Street*]

*Enter Duke Humphrey and his Men, in mourning
                cloaks.*

  Glo. Thus sometimes hath the brightest day a cloud;
And after summer evermore succeeds
Barren winter, with his wrathful nipping cold:
So cares and joys abound, as seasons fleet.   4
Sirs, what's o'clock?
  Serv.   Ten, my lord.
  Glo. Ten is the hour that was appointed me
To watch the coming of my punish'd duchess:
Uneath may she endure the flinty streets,   8
To tread them with her tender-feeling feet.
Sweet Nell, ill can thy noble mind abrook
The abject people, gazing on thy face
With envious looks still laughing at thy shame,   12
That erst did follow thy proud chariot wheels
When thou didst ride in triumph through the streets.
But, soft! I think she comes; and I'll prepare
My tear-stain'd eyes to see her miseries.   16

*Enter the Duchess in a white sheet, and a taper burn-
    ing in her hand, with the Sheriff, [Sir John Stan-
    ley,] and Officers.*

108 Which: *whom*   4 fleet: *pass*   8 Uneath: *hardly*
10 abrook: *endure*   11 abject: *vile*

Serv. So please your Grace, we'll take her from the
    sheriff.

Glo. No, stir not for your lives; let her pass by.

Elea. Come you, my lord, to see my open shame?
Now thou dost penance too. Look! how they gaze.   20
See! how the giddy multitude do point,
And nod their heads, and throw their eyes on thee.
Ah, Gloucester, hide thee from their hateful looks,
And, in thy closet pent up, rue my shame,   24
And ban thine enemies, both mine and thine!

    Glo. Be patient, gentle Nell; forget this grief.

    Elea. Ay, Gloucester, teach me to forget myself;
For whilst I think I am thy wedded wife,   28
And thou a prince, protector of this land,
Methinks I should not thus be led along,
Mail'd up in shame, with papers on my back,
And follow'd with a rabble that rejoice   32
To see my tears and hear my deep-fet groans.
The ruthless flint doth cut my tender feet,
And when I start, the envious people laugh,
And bid me be advised how I tread.   36
Ah, Humphrey! can I bear this shameful yoke?
Trowest thou that e'er I'll look upon the world,
Or count them happy that enjoys the sun?
No; dark shall be my light, and night my day;   40
To think upon my pomp shall be my hell.
Sometime I'll say, I am Duke Humphrey's wife;
And he a prince and ruler of the land:
Yet so he rul'd and such a prince he was   44
As he stood by whilst I, his forlorn duchess,
Was made a wonder and a pointing-stock

24 closet: *private apartment*	25 ban: *curse*
31 Mail'd: *wrapped*	32 with: *by*
33 deep-fet: *deep-drawn*	35 start: *wince*
36 advised: *cautious*	39 that enjoys: *who enjoy*
46 pointing-stock: *butt of ridicule*	

To every idle rascal follower.
But be thou mild and blush not at my shame;   48
Nor stir at nothing till the axe of death
Hang over thee, as, sure, it shortly will;
For Suffolk, he that can do all in all
With her that hateth thee, and hates us all,   52
And York, and impious Beaufort, that false priest,
Have all lim'd bushes to betray thy wings;
And, fly thou how thou canst, they'll tangle thee:
But fear not thou, until thy foot be snar'd,   56
Nor never seek prevention of thy foes.

   Glo. Ah, Nell! forbear: thou aimest all awry;
I must offend before I be attainted;
And had I twenty times so many foes,   60
And each of them had twenty times their power,
All these could not procure me any scath,
So long as I am loyal, true, and crimeless.
Wouldst have me rescue thee from this reproach?   64
Why, yet thy scandal were not wip'd away,
But I in danger for the breach of law.
Thy greatest help is quiet, gentle Nell:
I pray thee, sort thy heart to patience;   68
These few days' wonder will be quickly worn.

Enter a Herald.

   Her. I summon your Grace to his majesty's
parliament, holden at Bury the first of this
next month.   72
   Glo. And my consent ne'er ask'd herein before!
This is close dealing. Well, I will be there.
[Exit Herald.]

47 rascal follower: *worthless hireling*
37 prevention: *forestalling*   68 sort: *adapt*
62 scath: *injury*
71 Bury: *Bury St. Edmunds in Suffolk cf. n.*

54 *Cf. I. iii. 91*
59 attainted: *convicted*
69 worn: *worn away, expired* the first . . . month;
74 close: *secretive, sly*

My Nell, I take my leave: and, master sheriff,
Let not her penance exceed the king's commission.   7

   Sher. An 't please your Grace, here my commissio
     stays;
And Sir John Stanley is appointed now
To take her with him to the Isle of Man.

   Glo. Must you, Sir John, protect my lady here?   8

   Stan. So am I given in charge, may 't please you
     Grace.

   Glo. Entreat her not the worse in that I pray
You use her well.   The world may laugh again;
And I may live to do you kindness if   8
You do it her: and so, Sir John, farewell.

   Elea. What! gone, my lord, and bid me not farewell

   Glo. Witness my tears, I cannot stay to speak.

              Exit Gloucester [with his Men]

   Elea. Art thou gone too?   All comfort go with
     thee!   88
For none abides with me: my joy is death;
Death, at whose name I oft have been afear'd,
Because I wish'd this world's eternity.
Stanley, I prithee, go, and take me hence;   92
I care not whither, for I beg no favour,
Only convey me where thou art commanded.

   Stan. Why, madam, that is to the Isle of Man;
There to be us'd according to your state.   96

   Elea. That's bad enough, for I am but reproach:
And shall I then be us'd reproachfully?

   Stan. Like to a duchess, and Duke Humphrey's
     lady:
According to that state you shall be us'd.   100

   Elea. Sheriff, farewell, and better than I fare,

76 commission: *warrant*   77 stays: *stops*
91 this . . . eternity: *perpetuation of worldly enjoyment*
97 but reproach: *all disgrace*
101 better . . . fare: *may you fare better than I do*

lthough thou hast been conduct of my shame.

Sher. It is my office; and, madam, pardon me.

Elea. Ay, ay, farewell; thy office is discharg'd.   104
Come, Stanley, shall we go?

Stan. Madam, your penance done, throw off this
    sheet,
And go we to attire you for our journey.

Elea. My shame will not be shifted with my
    sheet: 108
No; it will hang upon my richest robes,
And show itself, attire me how I can.
Go, lead the way; I long to see my prison.   *Exeunt.*

ACT THIRD

Scene One

[The Abbey at Bury St. Edmunds]

*Sound a sennet. Enter King, Queen, Cardinal, Suf-
folk, York, Buckingham, Salisbury, and Warwick, to
the Parliament.*

King. I muse my Lord of Gloucester is not come:
'Tis not his wont to be the hindmost man,
Whate'er occasion keeps him from us now.

Queen. Can you not see? or will ye not observe   4
The strangeness of his alter'd countenance?
With what a majesty he bears himself,
How insolent of late he is become,
How proud, how peremptory, and unlike himself?   8
We know the time since he was mild and affable,
And if we did but glance a far-off look,

102 conduct: *the conductor*   1 muse: *wonder*
2 Cf. n.   9-12 Cf. n.   9 since: *when*

Immediately he was upon his knee,
That all the court admir'd him for submission: 1
But meet him now, and, be it in the morn,
When everyone will give the time of day,
He knits his brow and shows an angry eye,
And passeth by with stiff unbowed knee,   1
Disdaining duty that to us belongs.
Small curs are not regarded when they grin,
But great men tremble when the lion roars;
And Humphrey is no little man in England.   2
First note that he is near you in descent,
And should you fall, he is the next will mount.
Me seemeth then it is no policy,
Respecting what a rancorous mind he bears,   2
And his advantage following your decease,
That he should come about your royal person
Or be admitted to your highness' council.
By flattery hath he won the commons' hearts,   2
And when he please to make commotion,
'Tis to be fear'd they all will follow him.
Now 'tis the spring, and weeds are shallow-rooted;
Suffer them now and they'll o'ergrow the garden,   32
And choke the herbs for want of husbandry.
The reverent care I bear unto my lord
Made me collect these dangers in the duke.
If it be fond, call it a woman's fear;   36
Which fear if better reasons can supplant,
I will subscribe and say I wrong'd the duke.
My Lord of Suffolk, Buckingham, and York,
Reprove my allegation if you can   40

---

14 give . . . day: *say 'good morning'*   18 grin: *show their teeth*
23 policy: *prudent course*   24 Respecting: *considering*
25 *And considering the profit he would derive from your death*
33 husbandry: *cultivation of the soil*
35 collect: *infer*
36 fond: *foolish*
38 subscribe: *submit*
40 Reprove: *disprove*

Or else conclude my words effectual.

   Suf. Well hath your highness seen into this duke;
And had I first been put to speak my mind,
   think I should have told your Grace's tale.   **44**
The duchess, by his subornation,
Upon my life, began her devilish practices:
Or if he were not privy to those faults,
Yet, by reputing of his high descent,   **48**
As, next the king he was successive heir,
And such high vaunts of his nobility,
Did instigate the bedlam brain-sick duchess,
By wicked means to frame our sovereign's fall.   **52**
Smooth runs the water where the brook is deep,
And in his simple show he harbours treason.
The fox barks not when he would steal the lamb:
No, no, my sovereign; Gloucester is a man   **56**
Unsounded yet, and full of deep deceit.

   Car. Did he not, contrary to form of law,
Devise strange deaths for small offences done?

   York. And did he not, in his protectorship,   **60**
Levy great sums of money through the realm
For soldiers' pay in France, and never sent it?
By means whereof the towns each day revolted.

   Buck. Tut! these are petty faults to faults un-
     known,   **64**
Which time will bring to light in smooth Duke Hum-
     phrey.

   King. My lords, at once: the care you have of us,
To mow down thorns that would annoy our foot,
Is worthy praise; but shall I speak my conscience,   **68**
Our kinsman Gloucester is as innocent

---

41 effectual: *conclusive*   45 subornation: *instigation*
48 reputing: *boasting*   52 frame: *bring to pass*
59 Devise strange deaths; *cf. n.*   64 to: *in comparison with*
66 at once: *addressing you all together* (?), *without more ado* (?)
68 shall . . . conscience: *if I am to say what I really think*

From meaning treason to our royal person,
As is the sucking lamb or harmless dove.
The duke is virtuous, mild, and too well given   7
To dream on evil, or to work my downfall.

   Queen. Ah! what's more dangerous than this fon
     affiance!
Seems he a dove? his feathers are but borrow'd,
For he's disposed as the hateful raven: 7
Is he a lamb? his skin is surely lent him,
For he's inclin'd as is the ravenous wolf.
Who cannot steal a shape that means deceit?
Take heed, my lord; the welfare of us all   8
Hangs on the cutting short that fraudful man.

Enter Somerset.

   Som. All health unto my gracious sovereign!
   King. Welcome, Lord Somerset. What news from
     France?
   Som. That all your interest in those territories   8
Is utterly bereft you: all is lost.
   King. Cold news, Lord Somerset: but God's will be
     done!
   York. [*Aside.*] Cold news for me; for I had hope of
     France,
As firmly as I hope for fertile England.   8
Thus are my blossoms blasted in the bud,
And caterpillars eat my leaves away;
But I will remedy this gear ere long,
Or sell my title for a glorious grave.   92

Enter Gloucester.

   Glo. All happiness unto my lord the king!

72 too well given: *of too good character*
74 fond affiance: *foolish trust*   77 lent him: *i.e. not his own, false*
79 *What intending deceiver cannot assume a false appearance?*
83-85 *Cf. n.*   87 *Cold news for me; cf. n.*

Pardon, my liege, that I have stay'd so long.

Suf. Nay, Gloucester, know that thou art come too
  soon,

Unless thou wert more loyal than thou art: 96
  do arrest thee of high treason here.

Glo. Well, Suffolk, thou shalt not see me blush,
Nor change my countenance for this arrest:
A heart unspotted is not easily daunted.   100
The purest spring is not so free from mud
As I am clear from treason to my sovereign.
Who can accuse me? wherein am I guilty?

York. 'Tis thought, my lord, that you took bribes
  of France,   104
And, being protector, stay'd the soldiers' pay;
By means whereof his highness hath lost France.

Glo. Is it but thought so? What are they that think
  it?
I never robb'd the soldiers of their pay,   108
Nor ever had one penny bribe from France.
So help me God, as I have watch'd the night,
Ay, night by night, in studying good for England.
That doit that e'er I wrested from the king,   112
Or any groat I hoarded to my use,
Be brought against me at my trial-day!
No; many a pound of mine own proper store,
Because I would not tax the needy commons,   116
Have I dis-pursed to the garrisons,
And never ask'd for restitution.

Car. It serves you well, my lord, to say so much.

Glo. I say no more than truth, so help me God!   120

York. In your protectorship you did devise
Strange tortures for offenders, never heard of,

7 Cf. n.   110 watch'd: *kept vigil through*
12 doit: *Dutch coin, worth half a farthing*
13 groat: *four-penny coin*   117 dis-pursed: *paid out*

That England was defam'd by tyranny.

    Glo. Why, 'tis well known that, whiles I was pro­
tector,   12

Pity was all the fault that was in me;
For I should melt at an offender's tears,
And lowly words were ransom for their fault.
Unless it were a bloody murtherer,   12
Or foul felonious thief that fleec'd poor passengers,
I never gave them condign punishment:
Murther, indeed, that bloody sin, I tortur'd
Above the felon or what trespass else.   13

    Suf. My lord, these faults are easy, quickl­
answer'd:

But mightier crimes are laid unto your charge,
Whereof you cannot easily purge yourself.
I do arrest you in his highness' name,   13
And here commit you to my Lord Cardinal
To keep until your further time of trial.

    King. My Lord of Gloucester, 'tis my special hop­
That you will clear yourself from all suspect: 14
My conscience tells me you are innocent.

    Glo. Ah! gracious lord, these days are dangerous.
Virtue is chok'd with foul ambition,
And charity chas'd hence by rancour's hand;   14
Foul subornation is predominant,
And equity exil'd your highness' land.
I know their complot is to have my life;
And if my death might make this island happy,   14
And prove the period of their tyranny,
I would expend it with all willingness;
But mine is made the prologue to their play;

126 should: *was wont to, would*
129 passengers: *wayfarers*   130 condign: *adequat*
132 *Beyond any other kind of felony or misdemeanor*
138 further: *future*
145 subornation: *instigation to perjury or crime (cf. l. 45)*
149 period: *end*   150 it: *i.e. my lif*

'or thousands more, that yet suspect no peril,   152
Vill not conclude their plotted tragedy.
'eaufort's red sparkling eyes blab his heart's malice,
.nd Suffolk's cloudy brow his stormy hate;
harp Buckingham unburthens with his tongue   156
'he envious load that lies upon his heart;
.nd dogged York, that reaches at the moon,
Vhose overweening arm I have pluck'd back,
3y false accuse doth level at my life: 160
.nd you, my sovereign lady, with the rest,
'auseless have laid disgraces on my head,
.nd with your best endeavour have stirr'd up
Ny liefest liege to be mine enemy.   164
.y, all of you have laid your heads together;
Nyself had notice of your conventicles;
.nd all to make away my guiltless life.
shall not want false witness to condemn me,   168
Nor store of treasons to augment my guilt;
'he ancient proverb will be well effected:
A staff is quickly found to beat a dog.'

Car. My liege, his railing is intolerable.   172
f those that care to keep your royal person
'rom treason's secret knife and traitor's rage
3e thus upbraided, chid, and rated at,
And the offender granted scope of speech,   176
Twill make them cool in zeal unto your Grace.

Suf. Hath he not twit our sovereign lady here
With ignominious words, though clerkly couch'd,
As if she had suborned some to swear   180
False allegations to o'erthrow his state?

.53 conclude: *by their deaths bring to conclusion*
.59 overweening: *presumptuous; cf. n.*
.60 accuse: *accusation*   level: *aim*
.64 liefest liege: *dearest sovereign*
.66 conventicles: *secret meetings*   170 effected: *put into effect*
.73 care: *endure care, trouble themselves*   178 twit: *twitted*
.79 clerkly couch'd: *phrased with learned circumlocution*

Queen. But I can give the loser leave to chide.

Glo. Far truer spoke than meant: I lose, indeed;
Beshrew the winners, for they play'd me false!   1
And well such losers may have leave to speak.

Buck. He'll wrest the sense and hold us here all da
Lord Cardinal, he is your prisoner.

Car. Sirs, take away the duke, and guard hi
      sure.   1

Glo. Ah! thus King Henry throws away his crut
Before his legs be firm to bear his body:
Thus is the shepherd beaten from thy side,
And wolves are gnarling who shall gnaw thee first.
Ah! that my fear were false, ah! that it were;   1
For, good King Henry, thy decay I fear.

                        Exit Gloucester [*guarded*

King. My lords, what to your wisdoms seemeth bes
Do or undo, as if ourself were here.   19

Queen. What! will your highness leave the parlia
      ment?

King. Ay, Margaret; my heart is drown'd with grie
Whose flood begins to flow within mine eyes,
My body round engirt with misery,   20
For what's more miserable than discontent?
Ah! uncle Humphrey, in thy face I see
The map of honour, truth, and loyalty;
And yet, good Humphrey, is the hour to come   20
That e'er I prov'd thee false, or fear'd thy faith.
What low'ring star now envies thy estate,
That these great lords, and Margaret our queen,
Do seek subversion of thy harmless life?   20
Thou never didst them wrong, nor no man wrong;
And as the butcher takes away the calf,
And binds the wretch, and beats it when it strays,

184 Beshrew: *curse, fie on!*   192 gnarling: *snarling (to determine*
203 map: *epitome, abstract*

earing it to the bloody slaughter-house,   212
ven so, remorseless, have they borne him hence;
nd as the dam runs lowing up and down,
ooking the way her harmless young one went,
nd can do nought but wail her darling's loss;   216
ven so myself bewails good Gloucester's case,
Vith sad unhelpful tears, and with dimm'd eyes
ook after him, and cannot do him good;
o mighty are his vowed enemies.   220
Iis fortunes I will weep; and, 'twixt each groan,
ay 'Who's a traitor, Gloucester he is none.'   *Exit.*

   Queen. Free lords, cold snow melts with the sun's
            hot beams.
Ienry my lord is cold in great affairs,   224
'oo full of foolish pity; and Gloucester's show
Beguiles him as the mournful crocodile
Vith sorrow snares relenting passengers;
Dr as the snake, roll'd in a flowering bank,   228
Vith shining checker'd slough, doth sting a child
That for the beauty thinks it excellent.
Believe me, lords, were none more wise than I,—
And yet herein I judge mine own wit good,—   232
This Gloucester should be quickly rid the world,
To rid us from the fear we have of him.

   Car. That he should die is worthy policy;
And yet we want a colour for his death.   236
Tis meet he be condemn'd by course of law.

   Suf. But in my mind that were no policy:
The king will labour still to save his life;
The commons haply rise to save his life;   240
And yet we have but trivial argument,
More than mistrust, that shows him worthy death.

22 Who's: *whoever is*   223 Free: *noble*
29 slough: *skin*   236 colour: *pretext*
41 argument: *evidence*   242 mistrust: *suspicion*

York. So that, by this, you would not have him di

Suf. Ah, York, no man alive so fain as I.   2

York. 'Tis York that hath more reason for his deat

But, my Lord Cardinal, and you, my Lord of Suffol

Say as you think, and speak it from your souls,

Were 't not all one an empty eagle were set   2

To guard the chicken from a hungry kite,

As place Duke Humphrey for the king's protector?

Queen. So the poor chicken should be sure of deat

Suf. Madam, 'tis true: and were 't not madnes then,   2

To make the fox surveyor of the fold?

Who, being accus'd a crafty murtherer,

His guilt should be but idly posted over

Because his purpose is not executed.   2

No; let him die, in that he is a fox,

By nature prov'd an enemy to the flock,

Before his chaps be stain'd with crimson blood,

As Humphrey, prov'd by reasons, to my liege.   26

And do not stand on quillets how to slay him:

Be it by gins, by snares, by subtilty,

Sleeping or waking, 'tis no matter how,

So he be dead; for that is good deceit   26

Which mates him first that first intends deceit.

Queen. Thrice noble Suffolk, 'tis resolutely spoke.

Suf. Not resolute, except so much were done,

For things are often spoke and seldom meant;   26

But, that my heart accordeth with my tongue,

Seeing the deed is meritorious,

And to preserve my sovereign from his foe,

244 fain: *gladly*   248 empty: *i.e. starvin*
255 idly: *foolishly*   posted over: *passed over hastily, ignored*
260 prov'd: *i.e. proved an enemy*
261 stand on quillets: *waste time with subtle distinctions*
262 gins: *traps*   265 mates: *confounds, overwhelm*
269 that: *to prove that*

ay but the word and I will be his priest.   272

Car. But I would have him dead, my Lord of Suffolk,
re you can take due orders for a priest:
ay you consent and censure well the deed,
nd I'll provide his executioner;   276
tender so the safety of my liege.

Suf. Here is my hand, the deed is worthy doing.

Queen. And so say I.

York. And I: and now we three have spoke it,   280
: skills not greatly who impugns our doom.

Enter a Post.

Post. Great lords, from Ireland am I come amain,
'o signify that rebels there are up,
nd put the Englishmen unto the sword.   284
end succours, lords, and stop the rage betime,
efore the wound do grow uncurable;
'or, being green, there is great hope of help.

Car. A breach that craves a quick expedient stop! 288
Vhat counsel give you in this weighty cause?

York. That Somerset be sent as regent thither.
'is meet that lucky ruler be employ'd;
Vitness the fortune he hath had in France.   292

Som. If York, with all his far-fet policy,
Iad been the regent there instead of me,
Ie never would have stay'd in France so long.

York. No, not to lose it all, as thou hast done: 296
rather would have lost my life betimes
'han bring a burden of dishonour home,
}y staying there so long till all were lost.
how me one scar character'd on thy skin: 300

2 be his priest: *i.e. perform his last offices, arrange his death*
*7*5 censure well: *approve*   277 tender: *value*
*8*1 skills: *matters*   282 amain: *with speed*
*3*5 betime: *betimes, early*   288 expedient: *expeditious*
*9*3 far-fet: *far-fetched, cunning*   300 character'd: *written*

Men's flesh preserv'd so whole do seldom win.

    Queen. Nay then, this spark will prove a raging fir
If wind and fuel be brought to feed it with.
No more, good York; sweet Somerset, be still: 3
Thy fortune, York, hadst thou been regent there,
Might happily have prov'd far worse than his.

    York. What! worse than nought? nay, then a shan
    take all.

    Som. And in the number thee, that wishe
    shame.   3

    Car. My Lord of York, try what your fortune is.
Th' uncivil kerns of Ireland are in arms
And temper clay with blood of Englishmen:
To Ireland will you lead a band of men,   3
Collected choicely, from each county some,
And try your hap against the Irishmen?

    York. I will, my lord, so please his majesty.

    Suf. Why, our authority is his consent,   3
And what we do establish he confirms:
Then, noble York, take thou this task in hand.

    York. I am content: provide me soldiers, lords,
Whiles I take order for mine own affairs.   3

    Suf. A charge, Lord York, that I will see perform'
But now return we to the false Duke Humphrey.

    Car. No more of him; for I will deal with him
That henceforth he shall trouble us no more.   3
And so break off; the day is almost spent.
Lord Suffolk, you and I must talk of that event.

    York. My Lord of Suffolk, within fourteen days
At Bristow I expect my soldiers;   3
For there I'll ship them all for Ireland.

306 happily: *haply, perhaps*
308 in the number: *among the rest; cf. n.*
310 uncivil: *disorderly*   kerns: *light-armed irregulars*
311 temper clay: *moisten the ground*
318 *Cf. n.*

                       328 Bristow: *Brist*

Suf. I'll see it truly done, my Lord of York.

                       Exeunt. Manet York.

York. Now, York, or never, steel thy fearful
    thoughts,

And change misdoubt to resolution: 332

Be that thou hop'st to be, or what thou art

Resign to death; it is not worth th' enjoying.

Let pale-fac'd fear keep with the mean-born man,

And find no harbour in a royal heart.   336

Faster than spring-time showers comes thought on
    thought,

And not a thought but thinks on dignity.

My brain, more busy than the labouring spider,

Weaves tedious snares to trap mine enemies.   340

Well, nobles, well; 'tis politicly done,

To send me packing with an host of men:

I fear me you but warm the starved snake,

Who, cherish'd in your breasts, will sting your
    hearts.   344

'Twas men I lack'd, and you will give them me:

I take it kindly; yet be well assur'd

You put sharp weapons in a madman's hands.

Whiles I in Ireland nourish a mighty band,   348

I will stir up in England some black storm

Shall blow ten thousand souls to heaven or hell;

And this fell tempest shall not cease to rage

Until the golden circuit on my head,   352

Like to the glorious sun's transparent beams,

Do calm the fury of this mad-bred flaw.

And, for a minister of my intent,

331, 332 *Cf. n.*   342 send me packing: *pack me off*
343 starved: *frozen*   350 Shall: *which shall*
352 circuit: *circlet, crown*
354 mad-bred: *due to mad policies of Henry and his counselors*   flaw:
    squall of wind   355 minister: *agent*

I have seduc'd a headstrong Kentishman,   35

John Cade of Ashford,

To make commotion, as full well he can,

Under the title of John Mortimer.

In Ireland have I seen this stubborn Cade   36

Oppose himself against a troop of kerns,

And fought so long, till that his thighs with darts

Were almost like a sharp-quill'd porpentine:

And, in the end being rescu'd, I have seen   36

Him caper upright like a wild Morisco,

Shaking the bloody darts as he his bells.

Full often, like a shag-hair'd crafty kern,

Hath he conversed with the enemy,   36

And undiscover'd come to me again,

And given me notice of their villainies.

This devil here shall be my substitute;

For that John Mortimer, which now is dead,   37

In face, in gait, in speech, he doth resemble.

By this I shall perceive the commons' mind,

How they affect the house and claim of York.

Say he be taken, rack'd, and tortured,   376

I know no pain they can inflict upon him

Will make him say I mov'd him to those arms.

Say that he thrive,—as 'tis great like he will,—

Why, then from Ireland come I with my strength, 380

And reap the harvest which that rascal sow'd;

For, Humphrey being dead, as he shall be,

And Henry put apart, the next for me.   *Exit.*

356-359 *Cf. n.*   362 fought: *i.e. have seen him fight*
363 porpentine: *porcupine*
365 caper upright: *leap up and down*   Morisco: *morris-dancer*
367 shag-hair'd: *shaggy*   379 great like: *very likely*

Scene Two

[*Bury St. Edmunds. A Room in the Palace*]

Enter two or three [murderers] running over the stage,
from the murther of Duke Humphrey.

1. Mur. Run to my Lord of Suffolk; let him know
We have dispatch'd the duke, as he commanded.

2. Mur. O! that it were to do. What have we done?
Didst ever hear a man so penitent?   4

Enter Suffolk.

1. Mur. Here comes my lord.

Suf. Now, sirs, have you dispatch'd this thing?

1. Mur. Ay, my good lord, he's dead.

Suf. Why, that's well said. Go, get you to my
  house;   8
I will reward you for this venturous deed.
The king and all the peers are here at hand.
Have you laid fair the bed? is all things well,
According as I gave directions?   12

1. Mur. 'Tis, my good lord.

Suf. Away! be gone.   *Exeunt [Murderers].*

Sound trumpets. Enter the King, the Queen, Cardi-
  nal, Somerset, with Attendants.

King. Go, call our uncle to our presence straight;
Say, we intend to try his Grace to-day,   16
If he be guilty, as 'tis published.

Suf. I'll call him presently, my noble lord.   *Exit.*

King. Lords, take your places; and, I pray you all,
Proceed no straiter 'gainst our uncle Gloucester   20

3 to do: *i.e. still undone*   14 S. d.; *cf. n.*
17 If: *to determine whether*   published: *publicly asserted*
18 presently: *at once*   20 straiter: *more rigorously*

Than from true evidence, of good esteem,
He be approv'd in practice culpable.

Queen. God forbid any malice should prevail
That faultless may condemn a nobleman!   2
Pray God, he may acquit him of suspicion!

King. I thank thee, Meg; these words content m
   much.

Enter Suffolk.

How now! why look'st thou pale? why tremblest thou
Where is our uncle? what's the matter, Suffolk?   2

Suf. Dead in his bed, my lord; Gloucester is dead.

Queen. Marry, God forfend!

Car. God's secret judgment: I did dream to-night
The duke was dumb, and could not speak a word.   3

King swoons

Queen. How fares my lord?   Help, lords! the king
   is dead.

Som. Rear up his body; wring him by the nose.

Queen. Run, go, help, help!   O Henry, ope thine
   eyes!

Suf. He doth revive again.   Madam, be patient. 3

King. O heavenly God!

Queen.   How fares my gracious lord?

Suf. Comfort, my sovereign! gracious Henry, comfort!

King. What! doth my Lord of Suffolk comfort me?
Came he right now to sing a raven's note,   40
Whose dismal tune bereft my vital powers,
And thinks he that the chirping of a wren,
By crying comfort from a hollow breast,
Can chase away the first-conceived sound?   44
Hide not thy poison with such sugar'd words:

Lay not thy hands on me; forbear, I say:
Their touch affrights me as a serpent's sting.
Thou baleful messenger, out of my sight!   48
Upon thy eyeballs murderous tyranny
Sits in grim majesty to fright the world.
Look not upon me, for thine eyes are wounding:
Yet do not go away; come, basilisk,   52
And kill the innocent gazer with thy sight;
For in the shade of death I shall find joy,
In life but double death, now Gloucester's dead.

   Queen. Why do you rate my Lord of Suffolk thus? 56
Although the duke was enemy to him,
Yet he, most Christian-like, laments his death:
And for myself, foe as he was to me,
Might liquid tears or heart-offending groans   60
Or blood-consuming sighs recall his life,
I would be blind with weeping, sick with groans,
Look pale as primrose with blood-drinking sighs,
And all to have the noble duke alive.   64
What know I how the world may deem of me?
For it is known we were but hollow friends:
It may be judg'd I made the duke away:
So shall my name with slander's tongue be wounded, 68
And princes' courts be fill'd with my reproach.
This get I by his death. Ay me, unhappy!
To be a queen, and crown'd with infamy!

   King. Ah! woe is me for Gloucester, wretched
     man.   72

   Queen. Be woe for me, more wretched than he is.
What! dost thou turn away and hide thy face?
I am no loathsome leper; look on me.

49 murderous tyranny: *the tyranny of murder*
52 basilisk: *fabulous reptile whose sight caused death*
56 rate: *upbraid*   61 blood-consuming; *cf. n.*
66 hollow friends: *euphemism for enemies*   73 woe: *sorry*

What! art thou, like the adder, waxen deaf?   76
Be poisonous too and kill thy forlorn queen.
Is all thy comfort shut in Gloucester's tomb?
Why, then, Dame Margaret was ne'er thy joy:
Erect his statua and worship it,   80
And make my image but an alehouse sign.
Was I for this nigh wrack'd upon the sea,
And twice by awkward wind from England's bank
Drove back again unto my native clime?   84
What boded this, but well forewarning wind
Did seem to say, 'Seek not a scorpion's nest,
Nor set no footing on this unkind shore?'
What did I then, but curs'd the gentle gusts   88
And he that loos'd them forth their brazen caves;
And bid them blow towards England's blessed shore,
Or turn our stern upon a dreadful rock?
Yet Æolus would not be a murtherer,   92
But left that hateful office unto thee:
The pretty vaulting sea refus'd to drown me,
Knowing that thou wouldst have me drown'd on shore
With tears as salt as sea through thy unkindness: 96
The splitting rocks cower'd in the sinking sands,
And would not dash me with their ragged sides,
Because thy flinty heart, more hard than they,
Might in thy palace perish Margaret.   100
As far as I could ken thy chalky cliffs,
When from thy shore the tempest beat us back,
I stood upon the hatches in the storm,
And when the dusky sky began to rob   104
My earnest-gaping sight of thy land's view,
I took a costly jewel from my neck,
A heart it was, bound in with diamonds,

76 like the adder; *cf. n.*   waxen: *grown*
83 awkward: *unfavorable*   89 he: *i.e. Æolus*   forth: *out of*
90 bid: *I bade*   99 Because: *in order that*
100 perish: *destroy*   101 ken: *discern*

And threw it towards thy land: the sea receiv'd it,   108
And so I wish'd thy body might my heart:
And even with this I lost fair England's view,
And bid mine eyes be packing with my heart,
And call'd them blind and dusky spectacles   112
For losing ken of Albion's wished coast.
How often have I tempted Suffolk's tongue—
The agent of thy foul inconstancy—
To sit and witch me, as Ascanius did,   116
When he to madding Dido would unfold
His father's acts, commenc'd in burning Troy!
Am I not witch'd like her? or thou not false like him?
Ay me! I can no more. Die, Margaret!   120
For Henry weeps that thou dost live so long.

Noise within. Enter Warwick and many Commons.

War. It is reported, mighty sovereign,
That good Duke Humphrey traitorously is murder'd
By Suffolk and the Cardinal Beaufort's means.   124
The commons, like an angry hive of bees
That want their leader, scatter up and down,
And care not who they sting in his revenge.
Myself have calm'd their spleenful mutiny,   128
Until they hear the order of his death.

King. That he is dead, good Warwick, 'tis too true;
But how he died God knows, not Henry.
Enter his chamber, view his breathless corpse,   132
And comment then upon his sudden death.

War. That shall I do, my liege. Stay, Salisbury,
With the rude multitude till I return.   [*Exit.*]

King. O! thou that judgest all things, stay my
    thoughts,   136

111 be packing with: *accompany in flight*
112 spectacles: *visual organs*   116-118 *Cf. n.*
117 madding: *growing mad*   116 witch: *bewitch*
133 comment upon: *interpret*   129 order: *manner*
                                               134 Salisbury; *cf. n.*

My thoughts that labour to persuade my soul
Some violent hands were laid on Humphrey's life.
If my suspect be false, forgive me, God,
For judgment only doth belong to thee.   140
Fain would I go to chafe his paly lips
With twenty thousand kisses, and to drain
Upon his face an ocean of salt tears,
To tell my love unto his deaf dumb trunk,   144
And with my fingers feel his hand unfeeling:
But all in vain are these mean obsequies,

                              Bed put forth [by Warwick].
And to survey his dead and earthy image
What were it but to make my sorrow greater?   148

  War. Come hither, gracious sovereign, view this
       body.

  King. That is to see how deep my grave is made;
For with his soul fled all my worldly solace,
For seeing him I see my life in death.   152

  War. As surely as my soul intends to live
With that dread King that took our state upon him
To free us from his Father's wrathful curse,
I do believe that violent hands were laid   156
Upon the life of this thrice-famed duke.

  Suf. A dreadful oath, sworn with a solemn tongue!
What instance gives Lord Warwick for his vow?

  War. See how the blood is settled in his face.   160
Oft have I seen a timely-parted ghost,
Of ashy semblance, meagre, pale, and bloodless,
Being all descended to the labouring heart;
Who, in the conflict that it holds with death,   164
Attracts the same for aidance 'gainst the enemy;
Which with the heart there cools, and ne'er returneth

141 chafe: *warm*   paly: *pale*   146 obsequies: *acts of duty*
161 timely-parted ghost: *body of one whose soul has departed naturally*
163 Being: *i.e. the blood*

To blush and beautify the cheek again.
But see, his face is black and full of blood,   168
His eyeballs further out than when he liv'd,
Staring full ghastly like a strangled man;
His hair uprear'd, his nostrils stretch'd with strug-
     gling:
His hands abroad display'd, as one that grasp'd   172
And tugg'd for life, and was by strength subdu'd.
Look, on the sheets his hair, you see, is sticking;
His well-proportion'd beard made rough and rugged,
Like to the summer's corn by tempest lodg'd.   176
It cannot be but he was murder'd here;
The least of all these signs were probable.

     Suf. Why, Warwick, who should do the duke to
          death?
Myself and Beaufort had him in protection;   180
And we, I hope, sir, are no murtherers.

     War. But both of you were vow'd Duke Humphrey's
          foes,
And you, forsooth, had the good duke to keep:
'Tis like you would not feast him like a friend,   184
And 'tis well seen he found an enemy.

     Queen. Then you, belike, suspect these noblemen
As guilty of Duke Humphrey's timeless death.

     War. Who finds the heifer dead, and bleeding
          fresh,   188
And sees fast by a butcher with an axe,
But will suspect 'twas he that made the slaughter?
Who finds the partridge in the puttock's nest,
But may imagine how the bird was dead,   192
Although the kite soar with unbloodied beak?
Even so suspicious is this tragedy.

172 abroad display'd: *extended*   176 lodg'd: *beaten down*
178 probable: *sufficient as proof*   191 puttock's: *kite's, hawk's*

Queen. Are you the butcher, Suffolk? where's your
    knife?
Is Beaufort term'd a kite? where are his talons?   196
    Suf. I wear no knife to slaughter sleeping men;
But here's a vengeful sword, rusted with ease,
That shall be scoured in his rancorous heart
That slanders me with murther's crimson badge.   200
Say, if thou dar'st, proud Lord of Warwickshire,
That I am faulty in Duke Humphrey's death.
    War. What dares not Warwick, if false Suffolk dare
    him?   203
    Queen. He dares not calm his contumelious spirit,
Nor cease to be an arrogant controller,
Though Suffolk dare him twenty thousand times.
    War. Madam, be still, with reverence may I say;
For every word you speak in his behalf   208
Is slander to your royal dignity.
    Suf. Blunt-witted lord, ignoble in demeanour!
If ever lady wrong'd her lord so much,
Thy mother took into her blameful bed   212
Some stern untutor'd churl, and noble stock
Was graft with crab-tree slip; whose fruit thou art,
And never of the Nevils' noble race.
    War. But that the guilt of murther bucklers thee, 216
And I should rob the deathsman of his fee,
Quitting thee thereby of ten thousand shames,
And that my sovereign's presence makes me mild,
I would, false murd'rous coward, on thy knee   220
Make thee beg pardon for thy passed speech,
And say it was thy mother that thou meant'st;
That thou thyself wast born in bastardy:
And after all this fearful homage done,   224

205 controller: *meddling detractor*   217 deathsman: *executioner*
218 Quitting: *relieving*
224 fearful homage: *cowardly submission*

Give thee thy hire, and send thy soul to hell,
Pernicious blood-sucker of sleeping men.

Suf. Thou shalt be waking while I shed thy blood,
If from this presence thou dar'st go with me. 228

War. Away even now, or I will drag thee hence:
Unworthy though thou art, I'll cope with thee,
And do some service to Duke Humphrey's ghost.

Exeunt [Suffolk and Warwick].

King. What stronger breastplate than a heart un-
  tainted! 232
Thrice is he arm'd that hath his quarrel just,
And he but naked, though lock'd up in steel,
Whose conscience with injustice is corrupted.

A noise within.

Queen. What noise is this? 236

*Enter Suffolk and Warwick, with their weapons
drawn.*

King. Why, how now, lords! your wrathful weapons
  drawn
Here in our presence! dare you be so bold?
Why, what tumultuous clamour have we here?

Suf. The trait'rous Warwick, with the men of
  Bury, 240
Set all upon me, mighty sovereign.

Enter Salisbury.

Sal. [*Speaking to those within.*] Sirs, stand apart;
  the king shall know your mind.
Dread lord, the commons send you word by me,
Unless false Suffolk straight be done to death, 244
Or banished fair England's territories,
They will by violence tear him from your palace
And torture him with grievous lingering death.
They say, by him the good Duke Humphrey died; 248

They say, in him they fear your highness' death;
And mere instinct of love and loyalty,
Free from a stubborn opposite intent,
As being thought to contradict your liking,   252
Makes them thus forward in his banishment.
They say, in care of your most royal person,
That if your highness should intend to sleep,
And charge that no man should disturb your rest   256
In pain of your dislike or pain of death,
Yet, notwithstanding such a strait edict,
Were there a serpent seen, with forked tongue,
That slily glided towards your majesty,   260
It were but necessary you were wak'd,
Lest, being suffer'd in that harmful slumber,
The mortal worm might make the sleep eternal:
And therefore do they cry, though you forbid,   264
That they will guard you, whe'r you will or no,
From such fell serpents as false Suffolk is,
With whose envenomed and fatal sting,
Your loving uncle, twenty times his worth,   268
They say, is shamefully bereft of life.

    Commons within. An answer from the king, my Lord
of Salisbury!

    Suf. 'Tis like the commons, rude unpolish'd hinds,
Could send such message to their sovereign;   272
But you, my lord, were glad to be employ'd,
To show how quaint an orator you are:
But all the honour Salisbury hath won
Is that he was the lord ambassador,   276
Sent from a sort of tinkers to the king.

    Within. An answer from the king, or we will all
      break in!

250 mere instinct: *sincere impulse*
251 opposite intent: *purpose of opposition*
268 his worth: *as worthy as he*

265 whe'r: *whether*
274 quaint: *clever*

King. Go, Salisbury, and tell them all from me,
I thank them for their tender loving care; 280
And had I not been cited so by them,
Yet did I purpose as they do entreat;
For, sure, my thoughts do hourly prophesy
Mischance unto my state by Suffolk's means: 284
And therefore, by His majesty I swear,
Whose far-unworthy deputy I am,
He shall not breathe infection in this air
But three days longer, on the pain of death. 288
                    [*Exit Salisbury.*]

Queen. O Henry! let me plead for gentle Suffolk.
King. Ungentle queen, to call him gentle Suffolk!
No more, I say; if thou dost plead for him
Thou wilt but add increase unto my wrath. 292
Had I but said, I would have kept my word,
But when I swear, it is irrevocable.
[*To Suffolk.*] If after three days' space thou here
          be'st found
On any ground that I am ruler of, 296
The world shall not be ransom for thy life.
Come, Warwick, come, good Warwick, go with me;
I have great matters to impart to thee.
                    Exit [*with Warwick, etc.*].

Queen. Mischance and sorrow go along with you! 300
Heart's discontent and sour affliction
Be playfellows to keep you company!
There's two of you; the devil make a third,
And threefold vengeance tend upon your steps! 304
Suf. Cease, gentle queen, these execrations,
And let thy Suffolk take his heavy leave.
Queen. Fie, coward woman and soft-hearted wretch!
Hast thou not spirit to curse thine enemy? 308

281 cited: *urged*   287 breathe . . . in: *infect with his breath*
293 said: *affirmed without oath*

Suf. A plague upon them! Wherefore should I
    curse them?
Would curses kill, as doth the mandrake's groan,
I would invent as bitter-searching terms,
As curst, as harsh and horrible to hear,   312
Deliver'd strongly through my fixed teeth,
With full as many signs of deadly hate,
As lean-fac'd Envy in her loathsome cave.
My tongue should stumble in mine earnest words; 316
Mine eyes should sparkle like the beaten flint;
Mine hair be fix'd an end, as one distract;
Ay, every joint should seem to curse and ban:
And even now my burthen'd heart would break,   320
Should I not curse them. Poison be their drink!
Gall, worse than gall, the daintiest that they taste!
Their sweetest shade a grove of cypress trees!
Their chiefest prospect murd'ring basilisks!   324
Their softest touch as smart as lizard's stings!
Their music frightful as the serpent's hiss,
And boding screech-owls make the consort full!
All the foul terrors in dark-seated hell—   328
   Queen. Enough, sweet Suffolk; thou torment'st thy-
    self;
And these dread curses, like the sun 'gainst glass,
Or like an overcharged gun, recoil,
And turn the force of them upon thyself.   332
   Suf. You bade me ban, and will you bid me leave?
Now, by the ground that I am banish'd from,
Well could I curse away a winter's night,
Though standing naked on a mountain top,   336
Where biting cold would never let grass grow,

---

310 mandrake's groan; *cf. n.*   312 curst: *bitter*
318 an: *on*   as . . . distract: *like a madman's*
323 cypress trees: *trees symbolical of mourning*
325 smart: *painful*   327 consort: *band of musicians*
333 leave: *cease*

And think it but a minute spent in sport.
   Queen. O! let me entreat thee, cease! Give me thy
     hand,
That I may dew it with my mournful tears;   340
Nor let the rain of heaven wet this place,
To wash away my woeful monuments.
O! could this kiss be printed in thy hand,
                       [*Kisses his hand.*]
That thou might'st think upon these by the seal, 344
Through whom a thousand sighs are breath'd for thee.
So, get thee gone, that I may know my grief;
'Tis but surmis'd whiles thou art standing by,
As one that surfeits thinking on a want.   348
I will repeal thee, or, be well assur'd,
Adventure to be banished myself;
And banished I am, if but from thee.
Go; speak not to me; even now be gone.   352
O! go not yet. Even thus two friends condemn'd
Embrace and kiss, and take ten thousand leaves,
Loather a hundred times to part than die.
Yet now farewell; and farewell life with thee!   356
   Suf. Thus is poor Suffolk ten times banished,
Once by the king, and three times thrice by thee.
'Tis not the land I care for, wert thou thence;
A wilderness is populous enough,   360
So Suffolk had thy heavenly company:
For where thou art, there is the world itself,
With every several pleasure in the world,
And where thou art not, desolation.   364
I can no more: live thou to joy thy life;
Myself to joy in nought but that thou liv'st.

342 woeful monuments: *marks of woe (tear stains)*
344 seal: *impression of her lips; cf. n.*
348 *As when a glutton thinks of famine*
349 repeal thee: *secure your recall*   350 Adventure: *risk*

Enter Vaux.

   Queen. Whither goes Vaux so fast? what news, I
      prithee?

   Vaux. To signify unto his majesty   368
That Cardinal Beaufort is at point of death;
For suddenly a grievous sickness took him,
That makes him gasp and stare, and catch the air,
Blaspheming God, and cursing men on earth.   372
Sometime he talks as if Duke Humphrey's ghost
Were by his side; sometime he calls the king,
And whispers to his pillow, as to him,
The secrets of his overcharged soul: 376
And I am sent to tell his majesty
That even now he cries aloud for him.

   Queen. Go tell this heavy message to the king.
                                          Exit [*Vaux*].
Ay me! what is this world! what news are these!   380
But wherefore grieve I at an hour's poor loss,
Omitting Suffolk's exile, my soul's treasure?
Why only, Suffolk, mourn I not for thee,
And with the southern clouds contend in tears,   384
Theirs for the earth's increase, mine for my sorrows?
Now get thee hence: the king, thou know'st, is coming;
If thou be found by me thou art but dead.

   Suf. If I depart from thee I cannot live;   388
And in thy sight to die, what were it else
But like a pleasant slumber in thy lap?
Here could I breathe my soul into the air,
As mild and gentle as the cradle-babe,   392
Dying with mother's dug between its lips;
Where, from thy sight, I should be raging mad,
And cry out for thee to close up mine eyes,

369 *Cf. n.*   381 hour's poor loss: *petty transitory grief*
382 Omitting: *ignoring*   384 southern: *i.e. fog-laden*
387 by: *with*   393 its; *cf. n.*

To have thee with thy lips to stop my mouth: 396
So shouldst thou either turn my flying soul,
Or I should breathe it so into thy body,
And then it liv'd in sweet Elysium.
To die by thee were but to die in jest;   400
From thee to die were torture more than death.
O! let me stay, befall what may befall!
 Queen. Away! though parting be a fretful corro-
sive,
It is applied to a deathful wound.   404
To France, sweet Suffolk: let me hear from thee;
For wheresoe'er thou art in this world's globe,
I'll have an Iris that shall find thee out.
 Suf. I go.
 Queen. And take my heart with thee.   408
 Suf. A jewel, lock'd into the woefull'st cask
That ever did contain a thing of worth.
Even as a splitted bark, so sunder we:
This way fall I to death.
 Queen.   This way for me.   412
     Exeunt [at different doors].

Scene Three

[London. Cardinal Beaufort's Bedchamber]

*Enter the King, Salisbury, and Warwick to the
Cardinal in bed.*

King. How fares my lord? speak, Beaufort, to thy
sovereign.
Car. If thou be'st death, I'll give thee England's
treasure,

403 corrosive: *painful remedy* 407 Iris: *Juno's messenger*
409 into: *within* cask: *casket*

Enough to purchase such another island,
So thou wilt let me live, and feel no pain.   4
   King. Ah! what a sign it is of evil life
Where death's approach is seen so terrible.
   War. Beaufort, it is thy sovereign speaks to thee.
   Car. Bring me unto my trial when you will.   8
Died he not in his bed? where should he die?
Can I make men live whe'r they will or no?
O! torture me no more, I will confess.
Alive again? then show me where he is: 12
I'll give a thousand pound to look upon him.
He hath no eyes, the dust hath blinded them.
Comb down his hair; look! look! it stands upright,
Like lime-twigs set to catch my winged soul.   16
Give me some drink; and bid the apothecary
Bring the strong poison that I bought of him.
   King. O thou eternal Mover of the heavens!
Look with a gentle eye upon this wretch;   20
O! beat away the busy meddling fiend
That lays strong siege unto this wretch's soul,
And from his bosom purge this black despair.
   War. See how the pangs of death do make him
     grin!   24
   Sal. Disturb him not! let him pass peaceably.
   King. Peace to his soul, if God's good pleasure be!
Lord Cardinal, if thou think'st on heaven's bliss,
Hold up thy hand, make signal of thy hope.   28
He dies, and makes no sign. O God, forgive him!
   War. So bad a death argues a monstrous life.
   King. Forbear to judge, for we are sinners all.
Close up his eyes, and draw the curtain close;   32
And let us all to meditation.   *Exeunt.*

ACT FOURTH

Scene One

[Kent.   The Seashore near Dover]

*Alarum.   Fight at Sea.   Ordnance goes off.   Enter
   Lieutenant, Suffolk, and others [including Master,
   Master's Mate, Walter Whitmore, and various
   prisoners].*

Lieu. The gaudy, blabbing, and remorseful day
Is crept into the bosom of the sea,
And now loud-howling wolves arouse the jades
That drag the tragic melancholy night;   4
Who with their drowsy, slow, and flagging wings
Clip dead men's graves, and from their misty jaws
Breathe foul contagious darkness in the air.
Therefore bring forth the soldiers of our prize,   8
For, whilst our pinnace anchors in the Downs,
Here shall they make their ransom on the sand,
Or with their blood stain this discolour'd shore.
Master, this prisoner freely give I thee: 12
And thou that art his mate make boot of this;
The other [*Pointing to Suffolk*], Walter Whitmore, is
      thy share.

1. Gent. What is my ransom, master? let me know.

Mast. A thousand crowns, or else lay down your
      head.   16

Mate. And so much shall you give, or off goes yours.

Lieu. What! think you much to pay two thousand
      crowns,

1-7 *Cf. n.*   6 Clip: *embrace*
9 pinnace: *one-masted vessel*   Downs; *cf. n.*
11 discolour'd; *cf. n.*
13 make . . . this: *take your profit from the ransom of this one*

And bear the name and port of gentlemen?

Cut both the villains' throats! for die you shall: 20

The lives of those which we have lost in fight

Be counterpois'd with such a petty sum!

   1. Gent. I'll give it, sir; and therefore spare my life.

   2. Gent. And so will I, and write home for it

      straight.   24

   Whit. I lost mine eye in laying the prize aboard,

[*To Suffolk.*] And therefore to revenge it shalt thou

    die;

And so should these if I might have my will.

   Lieu. Be not so rash: take ransom; let him live.   28

   Suf. Look on my George; I am a gentleman:

Rate me at what thou wilt, thou shalt be paid.

   Whit. And so am I; my name is Walter Whitmore.

How now! why start'st thou? what! doth death

    affright?   32

   Suf. Thy name affrights me, in whose sound is

    death.

A cunning man did calculate my birth,

And told me that by *Water* I should die:

Yet let not this make thee be bloody-minded;   36

Thy name is Gaultier, being rightly sounded.

   Whit. Gaultier, or Walter, which it is I care not.

Never yet did base dishonour blur our name

But with our sword we wip'd away the blot: 40

Therefore, when merchant-like I sell revenge,

Broke be my sword, my arms torn and defac'd,

And I proclaim'd a coward through the world!

   Suf. Stay, Whitmore; for thy prisoner is a prince, 44

The Duke of Suffolk, William de la Pole.

   Whit. The Duke of Suffolk muffled up in rags!

---

19 port: *demeanor*   22 counterpois'd: *balanced, reckoned equal*
25 laying aboard: *grappling with*   29 George; *cf. n.*
30 Rate me: *set my ransom*   35 Water; *cf. n.*

Suf. Ay, but these rags are no part of the duke:
Jove sometime went disguis'd, and why not I ?   48
  Lieu. But Jove was never slain, as thou shalt be.
  Suf. Obscure and lowly swain, King Henry's blood,
The honourable blood of Lancaster,
Must not be shed by such a jaded groom.   52
Hast thou not kiss'd thy hand and held my stirrup ?
Bare-headed plodded by my foot-cloth mule,
And thought thee happy when I shook my head ?
How often hast thou waited at my cup,   56
Fed from my trencher, kneel'd down at the board,
When I have feasted with Queen Margaret ?
Remember it and let it make thee crest-fall'n ;
Ay, and allay this thy abortive pride.   60
How in our voiding lobby hast thou stood
And duly waited for my coming forth ?
This hand of mine hath writ in thy behalf,
And therefore shall it charm thy riotous tongue.   64
  Whit. Speak, captain, shall I stab the forlorn swain ?
  Lieu. First let my words stab him, as he hath me.
  Suf. Base slave, thy words are blunt, and so art thou.
  Lieu. Convey him hence, and on our longboat's
    side   68
Strike off his head.
  Suf.   Thou dar'st not for thy own.
  Lieu. Yes, Pole.
  Suf.   Pole !
  Lieu.   Pool ! Sir Pool ! lord !
Ay, kennel, puddle, sink ; whose filth and dirt
Troubles the silver spring where England drinks.   72
Now will I dam up this thy yawning mouth

48-50 *Cf. n.*   50 King Henry's blood; *cf. n.*
52 jaded: *contemptible*   54 foot-cloth mule; *cf. n.*
61 voiding lobby: *antechamber*   71 kennel: *gutter*   sink: *cesspool*

For swallowing the treasure of the realm:
Thy lips, that kiss'd the queen, shall sweep the ground;
And thou, that smil'dst at good Duke Humphrey's
    death, 76
Against the senseless winds shalt grin in vain,
Who in contempt shall hiss at thee again:
And wedded be thou to the hags of hell,
For daring to affy a mighty lord 80
Unto the daughter of a worthless king,
Having neither subject, wealth, nor diadem.
By devilish policy art thou grown great,
And, like ambitious Sylla, overgorg'd 84
With gobbets of thy mother's bleeding heart.
By thee Anjou and Maine were sold to France,
The false revolting Normans thorough thee
Disdain to call us lord, and Picardy 88
Hath slain their governors, surpris'd our forts,
And sent the ragged soldiers wounded home.
The princely Warwick, and the Nevils all,
Whose dreadful swords were never drawn in vain, 92
As hating thee, are rising up in arms:
And now the house of York, thrust from the crown
By shameful murther of a guiltless king,
And lofty proud encroaching tyranny, 96
Burns with revenging fire; whose hopeful colours
Advance our half-fac'd sun, striving to shine,
Under the which is writ *Invitis nubibus.*
The commons here in Kent are up in arms; 100
And to conclude, reproach and beggary
Is crept into the palace of our king,
And all by thee. Away! convey him hence.

---

74 For: *for fear of, to prevent*   80 affy: *betroth*
84 ambitious Sylla: *cf n.*   85 gobbets: *lumps of flesh*
87 thorough: *through*   95 guiltless king: *i.e. Richard II*
98 Advance: *display*   half-fac'd· *with disk half obscured; cf. n.*
99 Invitis nubibus: *in spite of clouds*

Suf. O! that I were a god, to shoot forth thunder   104
Upon these paltry, servile, abject drudges.
Small things make base men proud: this villain here,
Being captain of a pinnace, threatens more
Than Bargulus, the strong Illyrian pirate.   108
Drones suck not eagles' blood, but rob beehives.
It is impossible that I should die
By such a lowly vassal as thyself.
Thy words move rage, and not remorse in me: 112
I go of message from the queen to France;
I charge thee, waft me safely cross the Channel.

    Lieu. Walter!

    Whit. Come, Suffolk, I must waft thee to thy death.

    Suf. Pene gelidus timor occupat artus: it is thee I
    fear.   117

    Whit. Thou shalt have cause to fear before I leave
    thee.
What! are ye daunted now? now will ye stoop?

    1. Gent. My gracious lord, entreat him, speak him
    fair.   120

    Suf. Suffolk's imperial tongue is stern and rough,
Us'd to command, untaught to plead for favour.
Far be it we should honour such as these
With humble suit: no, rather let my head   124
Stoop to the block than these knees bow to any,
Save to the God of heaven and to my king;
And sooner dance upon a bloody pole
Than stand uncover'd to the vulgar groom.   128
True nobility is exempt from fear:
More can I bear than you dare execute.

    Lieu. Hale him away, and let him talk no more.

    Suf. Come, soldiers, show what cruelty ye can,   132

---

108 Bargulus; *cf. n.*   113 of message: *as messenger*
114 waft: *convey by water*   117 Pene . . . artus; *cf. n.*
127 dance . . . pole; *cf. n.*

That this my death may never be forgot.
Great men oft die by vile besonians.
A Roman sworder and banditto slave
Murder'd sweet Tully; Brutus' bastard hand   136
Stabb'd Julius Cæsar; savage islanders
Pompey the Great; and Suffolk dies by pirates.

               Exit Walter with Suffolk.

   Lieu. And as for these whose ransom we have set,
It is our pleasure one of them depart: 140
Therefore come you with us and let him go.

   Exit Lieutenant, and the rest. Manet the first Gent.

   Enter Walter with the body [*of Suffolk*].

   Whit. There let his head and lifeless body lie,
Until the queen his mistress bury it.   *Exit Walter.*
   1. Gent. O barbarous and bloody spectacle!   144
His body will I bear unto the king:
If he revenge it not, yet will his friends;
So will the queen, that living held him dear.

                    [*Exit with the body.*]

Scene Two

[*Blackheath*]

Enter Bevis and John Holland.

   Bevis. Come, and get thee a sword, though
made of a lath: they have been up these two
days.

   Holl. They have the more need to sleep now   4
then.

   Bevis. I tell thee, Jack Cade the clothier means

134 besonians: *beggars*   135 sworder: *gladiator*
137 savage islanders; *cf. n.*   2 up: *in arms*
6 clothier: *cloth-worker*

to dress the commonwealth, and turn it, and set
a new nap upon it.   8

Holl. So he had need, for 'tis threadbare.
Well, I say it was never merry world in England
since gentlemen came up.

Bevis. O miserable age! Virtue is not regarded 12
in handicraftsmen.

Holl. The nobility think scorn to go in
leather aprons.

Bevis. Nay, more; the king's council are no 16
good workmen.

Holl. True; and yet it is said, 'Labour in thy
vocation': which is as much to say as, let the
magistrates be labouring men; and therefore 20
should we be magistrates.

Bevis. Thou hast hit it; for there's no better
sign of a brave mind than a hard hand.

Holl. I see them! I see them! There's 24
Best's son, the tanner of Wingham,—

Bevis. He shall have the skins of our enemies
to make dog's-leather of.

Holl. And Dick the butcher,—   28

Bevis. Then is sin struck down like an ox, and
iniquity's throat cut like a calf.

Holl. And Smith the weaver,—

Bevis. *Argo,* their thread of life is spun.   32

Holl. Come, come, let's fall in with them.

Drum.   *Enter Cade, Dick Butcher, Smith the Weaver,
and a Sawyer, with infinite numbers.*

Cade. We John Cade, so termed of our supposed father,—

11 came up: *came into fashion*   32 Argo: *ergo, therefore*

Butch. [*Aside.*] Or rather, of stealing a cade 36 of herrings.

Cade. For our enemies shall fall before us, inspired with the spirit of putting down kings and princes,—Command silence.   40

Butch. Silence!

Cade. My father was a Mortimer,—

Butch. [*Aside.*] He was an honest man, and a good bricklayer.   44

Cade. My mother a Plantagenet,—

Butch. [*Aside.*] I knew her well; she was a midwife.

Cade. My wife descended of the Lacies,— 48

Butch. [*Aside.*] She was, indeed, a pedlar's daughter, and sold many laces.

Weav. [*Aside.*] But now of late, not able to travel with her furred pack, she washes bucks 52 here at home.

Cade. Therefore am I of an honourable house.

Butch. [*Aside.*] Ay, by my faith, the field is 56 honourable; and there was he born, under a hedge; for his father had never a house but the cage.

Cade. Valiant I am.   60

Weav. [*Aside.*] A' must needs, for beggary is valiant.

Cade. I am able to endure much.

Butch. [*Aside.*] No question of that, for I have 64 seen him whipped three market-days together.

Cade. I fear neither sword nor fire.

36 cade: *barrel (containing 600 herrings)*
38 For: *because*   fall: *pun on Latin 'cado' meaning fall*
48 Lacies: *family name of the Earls of Lincoln*
52 furred pack: *waterproof pack, made of skin with the hair outward* washes bucks: *takes in washing*
59 cage: *lock-up*   51 A' must needs: *he must be*

Weav. [*Aside.*] He need not fear the sword, for his coat is of proof.   68

Butch. [*Aside.*] But methinks he should stand in fear of fire, being burnt i' the hand for stealing of sheep.

Cade. Be brave, then; for your captain is 72 brave, and vows reformation.   There shall be in England seven halfpenny loaves sold for a penny; the three-hooped pot shall have ten hoops; and I will make it felony to drink small 76 beer.   All the realm shall be in common, and in Cheapside shall my palfrey go to grass.   And when I am king,—as king I will be,—

All. God save your majesty!   80

Cade. I thank you, good people:—there shall be no money; all shall eat and drink on my score; and I will apparel them all in one livery, that they may agree like brothers, and worship 84 me their lord.

Butch. The first thing we do, let's kill all the lawyers.

Cade. Nay, that I mean to do.   Is not this 88 a lamentable thing, that of the skin of an innocent lamb should be made parchment? that parchment, being scribbled o'er, should undo a man?   Some say the bee stings; but I say, 'tis 92 the bee's wax, for I did but seal once to a thing, and I was never mine own man since.   How now! who's there?

Enter a Clerk.

68 of proof: *tried by long service*
73 reformation: *alteration of government*
75 three-hooped pot: *wooden quart-pot*
82, 83 on my score: *at my expense*
86, 87 kill . . . lawyers; *cf. n.*

Weav. The clerk of Chatham: he can write 96
and read and cast accompt.

Cade. O monstrous!

Weav. We took him setting of boys' copies.

Cade. Here's a villain!   100

Weav. Has a book in his pocket with red
letters in 't.

Cade. Nay, then he is a conjurer.

Butch. Nay, he can make obligations, and 104
write court-hand.

Cade. I am sorry for 't: the man is a proper
man, of mine honour; unless I find him guilty,
he shall not die. Come hither, sirrah, I must 108
examine thee. What is thy name?

Clerk. Emmanuel.

Butch. They use to write it on the top of
letters. 'Twill go hard with you.   112

Cade. Let me alone. Dost thou use to write
thy name, or hast thou a mark to thyself, like
a honest plain-dealing man?

Clerk. Sir, I thank God, I have been so well 116
brought up, that I can write my name.

All. He hath confessed: away with him! he's
a villain and a traitor.

Cade. Away with him, I say: hang him with 120
his pen and ink-horn about his neck.

Exit one with the Clerk.

Enter Michael.

Mich. Where's our general?

Cade. Here I am, thou particular fellow.

---

97 cast accompt: *calculate*   99 copies: *models of handwriting*
104 obligations: *contracts*
105 court-hand: *type of handwriting used in legal documents*
106 proper: *good-looking*   111, 112 They . . . letters; *cf. n*
123 particular: *as opposed to 'general'*

Mich. Fly, fly, fly! Sir Humphrey Stafford 124
and his brother are hard by, with the king's
forces.

Cade. Stand, villain, stand, or I'll fell thee
down. He shall be encountered with a man as 128
good as himself: he is but a knight, is a'?

Mich. No.

Cade. To equal him, I will make myself a
knight presently. [*Kneels.*] Rise up Sir John 132
Mortimer. [*Rises.*] Now have at him.

*Enter Sir Humphrey Stafford and his Brother, with
drum and Soldiers.*

Staf. Rebellious hinds, the filth and scum of Kent,
Mark'd for the gallows, lay your weapons down;
Home to your cottages, forsake this groom: 136
The king is merciful, if you revolt.

Bro. But angry, wrathful, and inclin'd to blood,
If you go forward: therefore yield, or die.

Cade. As for these silken-coated slaves, I pass
    not: 140
It is to you, good people, that I speak,
O'er whom, in time to come I hope to reign;
For I am rightful heir unto the crown.

Staf. Villain! thy father was a plasterer;   144
And thou thyself a shearman, art thou not?

Cade. And Adam was a gardener.

Bro. And what of that?

Cade. Marry, this: Edmund Mortimer, Earl of
    March,   148
Married the Duke of Clarence' daughter, did he not?

Staf. Ay, sir.

Cade. By her he had two children at one birth.

30 No: *i.e. he is no more*   137 revolt: *i.e. forsake Cade*
45 shearman: *one who shears cloth*

Bro. That's false. 152

Cade. Ay, there's the question; but I say, 'tis true:
The elder of them, being put to nurse,
Was by a beggar-woman stol'n away;
And, ignorant of his birth and parentage, 156
Became a bricklayer when he came to age:
His son am I; deny it if you can.

Butch. Nay, 'tis too true; therefore he shall be king.

Weav. Sir, he made a chimney in my father's 160
house, and the bricks are alive at this day to
testify it; therefore deny it not.

Staf. And will you credit this base drudge's words,
That speaks he knows not what? 164

All. Ay, marry, will we; therefore get ye gone.

Bro. Jack Cade, the Duke of York hath taught you
this.

Cade. [*Aside.*] He lies, for I invented it myself. Go to, sirrah; tell the king from me, that, 168
for his father's sake, Henry the Fifth, in whose
time boys went to span-counter for French
crowns, I am content he shall reign; but I'll be
protector over him. 172

Butch. And furthermore, we'll have the Lord
Say's head for selling the dukedom of Maine.

Cade. And good reason; for thereby is England mained, and fain to go with a staff, but 176
that my puissance holds it up. Fellow kings, I
tell you that that Lord Say hath gelded the
commonwealth, and made it an eunuch; and
more than that, he can speak French; and 180
therefore he is a traitor.

Staf. O gross and miserable ignorance!

Cade. Nay, answer, if you can: the French-

70 span-counter: *children's game played with coins or counters*
176 mained: *maimed*

men are our enemies; go to then, I ask but 184
this: can he that speaks with the tongue of an
enemy be a good counsellor, or no?

All. No, no; and therefore we'll have his head.

Bro. Well, seeing gentle words will not prevail,   188
Assail them with the army of the king.

Staf. Herald, away; and throughout every town
Proclaim them traitors that are up with Cade;
That those which fly before the battle ends   192
May, even in their wives' and children's sight,
Be hang'd up for example at their doors:
And you, that be the king's friends, follow me.

     Exit [with Brother and Soldiers].

Cade. And you, that love the commons, follow
 me.   196
Now show yourselves men; 'tis for liberty.
We will not leave one lord, one gentleman:
Spare none but such as go in clouted shoon,
For they are thrifty honest men, and such   200
As would, but that they dare not, take our parts.

Butch. They are all in order, and march toward us.

Cade. But then are we in order when we are
most out of order. Come, march! forward!   204

       [Exeunt.]

Scene Three

[Another Part of Blackheath]

*Alarums to the fight, wherein both the Staffords are
slain. Enter Cade and the rest.*

 Cade. Where's Dick, the butcher of Ashford?
 Butch. Here, sir.
 Cade. They fell before thee like sheep and

99 clouted shoon: *patched (?), hobnailed (?) shoes*

oxen, and thou behavedst thyself as if thou 4
hadst been in thine own slaughter-house: therefore thus will I reward thee; the Lent shall be
as long again as it is, and thou shalt have a
licence to kill for a hundred lacking one. 8

Butch. I desire no more.

Cade. And, to speak truth, thou deserv'st no
less. This monument of the victory will I bear;
[*Puts on Sir Humphrey Stafford's armour.*]
and the bodies shall be dragged at my horse' 12
heels, till I do come to London, where we will
have the Mayor's sword borne before us.

Butch. If we mean to thrive and do good,
break open the gaols and let out the prisoners. 16

Cade. Fear not that, I warrant thee. Come;
let's march towards London. *Exeunt.*

Scene Four

[*London. A Room in the Palace*]

*Enter the King with a supplication, and the Queen
with Suffolk's head; the Duke of Buckingham, and
the Lord Say.*

Queen. Oft have I heard that grief softens the mind
And makes it fearful and degenerate;
Think therefore on revenge, and cease to weep.
But who can cease to weep and look on this?
Here may his head lie on my throbbing breast;
But where's the body that I should embrace?

Buck. What answer makes your Grace to the
rebels' supplication?

King. I'll send some holy bishop to entreat;

8 licence to kill; *cf. n.*   17 Fear: *doul*

For God forbid so many simple souls
Should perish by the sword! And I myself,
Rather than bloody war shall cut them short,   12
Will parley with Jack Cade their general.
But stay, I'll read it over once again.

   Queen. Ah, barbarous villains! hath this lovely face
Rul'd like a wandering planet over me,   16
And could it not enforce them to relent,
That were unworthy to behold the same?

   King. Lord Say, Jack Cade hath sworn to have thy
     head.

   Say. Ay, but I hope your highness shall have his.   20

   King. How now, madam!
Still lamenting and mourning for Suffolk's death?
I fear me, love, if that I had been dead,
Thou wouldest not have mourn'd so much for me. 24

   Queen. No, my love; I should not mourn, but die
     for thee.

Enter a Messenger.

   King. How now! what news? why com'st thou
     in such haste?

   Mess. The rebels are in Southwark; fly, my lord!
Jack Cade proclaims himself Lord Mortimer,   28
Descended from the Duke of Clarence' house,
And calls your Grace usurper openly,
And vows to crown himself in Westminster.
His army is a ragged multitude   32
Of hinds and peasants, rude and merciless:
Sir Humphrey Stafford and his brother's death
Hath given them heart and courage to proceed.
All scholars, lawyers, courtiers, gentlemen,   36
They call false caterpillars, and intend their death.

16 like . . . planet: *alluding to planetary influence*
33 hinds: *farm laborers*

King. O graceless men! they know not what they
do.

Buck. My gracious lord, retire to Killingworth,
Until a power be rais'd to put them down.   40

Queen. Ah! were the Duke of Suffolk now alive,
These Kentish rebels would be soon appeas'd.

King. Lord Say, the traitors hate thee,
Therefore away with us to Killingworth.   44

Say. So might your Grace's person be in danger.
The sight of me is odious in their eyes;
And therefore in this city will I stay,
And live alone as secret as I may.   48

Enter another Messenger.

Mess. Jack Cade hath gotten London bridge;
The citizens fly and forsake their houses;
The rascal people, thirsting after prey,
Join with the traitor; and they jointly swear   52
To spoil the city and your royal court.

Buck. Then linger not, my lord; away! take horse.

King. Come, Margaret; God, our hope, will succour
us.

Queen. My hope is gone, now Suffolk is deceas'd. 56

King. [*To Lord Say.*] Farewell, my lord: trust not
the Kentish rebels.

Buck. Trust nobody, for fear you be betray'd.

Say. The trust I have is in mine innocence,
And therefore am I bold and resolute.   *Exeunt.*

39 Killingworth: *Kenilworth Castle in Warwickshire*
42 appeas'd: *pacified, reduced to quiet*   51 rascal people: *rabble*

Scene Five

[The Same.   The Tower]

Enter Lord Scales upon the Tower walking.   Then enter two or three Citizens below.

Scales. How now! is Jack Cade slain?

1. Cit. No, my lord, nor likely to be slain;
for they have won the bridge, killing all those
that withstand them.   The Lord Mayor craves   4
aid of your honour from the Tower, to defend
the city from the rebels.

Scales. Such aid as I can spare you shall command;
But I am troubled here with them myself;   8
The rebels have assay'd to win the Tower.
But get you to Smithfield and gather head,
And thither I will send you Matthew Goffe:
Fight for your king, your country, and your lives; 12
And so, farewell, for I must hence again.   *Exeunt.*

Scene Six

[London.   Cannon Street]

Enter Jack Cade and the rest, and strikes his staff on London-stone.

Cade. Now is Mortimer lord of this city.   And
here, sitting upon London-stone, I charge and
command that, of the city's cost, the pissing-
conduit run nothing but claret wine this first   4
year of our reign.   And now, henceforward, it

10 gather head: *collect your forces*
2 London-stone: *a Roman milestone in Cannon Street*
3, 4 pissing-conduit: *a small water fountain*

shall be treason for any that calls me other than Lord Mortimer.

Enter a Soldier, running.

Sold. Jack Cade! Jack Cade!   8
Cade. Knock him down there.

They kill him.

Smith. If this fellow be wise, he'll never call ye Jack Cade more: I think he hath a very fair warning.   12

Dick. My lord, there's an army gathered together in Smithfield.

Cade. Come then, let's go fight with them. But first, go and set London-bridge on fire, and, 16 if you can, burn down the Tower too. Come, let's away.   *Exeunt omnes.*

Scene Seven

[*The Same. Smithfield*]

Alarums. Matthew Goffe is slain, and all the rest [of the King's forces]. Then enter Jack Cade, with his Company.

Cade. So, sirs:—Now go some and pull down the Savoy; others to the inns of court: down with them all.

Dick. I have a suit unto your lordship.   4

Cade. Be it a lordship, thou shalt have it for that word.

Dick. Only that the laws of England may come out of your mouth.   8

Holl. [*Aside.*] Mass, 'twill be sore law then;

2 Savoy: *the London residence of the Duke of Lancaster*   inns of
court: *the abode of lawyers*

for he was thrust in the mouth with a spear,
and 'tis not whole yet.

Smith. [*Aside.*] Nay, John, it will be stink- 12
ing law; for his breath stinks with eating
toasted cheese.

Cade. I have thought upon it; it shall be so.
Away! burn all the records of the realm: my 16
mouth shall be the parliament of England.

Holl. [*Aside.*] Then we are like to have
biting statutes, unless his teeth be pulled out.

Cade. And henceforward all things shall be 20
in common.

Enter a Messenger.

Mess. My lord, a prize, a prize! here's the
Lord Say, which sold the towns in France; he
that made us pay one-and-twenty fifteens, and 24
one shilling to the pound, the last subsidy.

Enter George [Bevis] with the Lord Say.

Cade. Well, he shall be beheaded for it ten
times. Ah! thou say, thou serge, nay, thou
buckram lord; now art thou within point- 28
blank of our jurisdiction regal. What canst
thou answer to my majesty for giving up of
Normandy unto Monsieur Basimecu, the Dauphin of France? Be it known unto thee by 32
these presence, even the presence of Lord Mortimer, that I am the besom that must sweep
the court clean of such filth as thou art. Thou
hast most traitorously corrupted the youth of 36
the realm in erecting a grammar-school; and

23 which . . . France; *cf. n.*   24 one-and-twenty fifteens; *cf. n.*
27, 28 say . . . serge . . . buckram: *various kinds of cloth*
31 Basimecu: *obscene term of derision*
33 these presence: *humorous error for 'these presents'*
34 besom: *broom*

whereas, before, our forefathers had no other
books but the score and the tally, thou hast
caused printing to be used; and, contrary to 40
the king his crown and dignity, thou hast built
a paper-mill. It will be proved to thy face that
thou hast men about thee that usually talk of
a noun and a verb, and such abominable words 44
as no Christian ear can endure to hear. Thou
hast appointed justices of peace, to call poor
men before them about matters they were not
able to answer. Moreover, thou hast put them 48
in prison; and because they could not read,
thou hast hanged them; when indeed only for
that cause they have been most worthy to live.
Thou dost ride in a foot-cloth, dost thou not? 52

Say. What of that?

Cade. Marry, thou ought'st not to let thy
horse wear a cloak, when honester men than
thou go in their hose and doublets.   56

Dick. And work in their shirt too; as myself,
for example, that am a butcher.

Say. You men of Kent,—

Dick. What say you of Kent?   60

Say. Nothing but this: 'tis *bona terra, mala gens.*

Cade. Away with him! away with him! he
speaks Latin.

Say. Hear me but speak, and bear me where you
will.   64

Kent, in the Commentaries Cæsar writ,
Is term'd the civil'st place of all this isle:
Sweet is the country, because full of riches;
The people liberal, valiant, active, wealthy;   68

39 the score and the tally; *cf. n.*   40 printing; *cf. n.*
41 king his: *king's*   43 usually: *habitually*
49 because . . . . read: *lacking 'benefit of clergy'*
56 hose and doublets; *cf. n.*   65, 66 *Cf. n.*

Which makes me hope you are not void of pity.
I sold not Maine, I lost not Normandy;
Yet, to recover them, would lose my life.
Justice with favour have I always done;   72
Prayers and tears have mov'd me, gifts could never.
When have I aught exacted at your hands,
But to maintain the king, the realm, and you?
Large gifts have I bestow'd on learned clerks,   76
Because my book preferr'd me to the king,
And seeing ignorance is the curse of God,
Knowledge the wing wherewith we fly to heaven,
Unless you be possess'd with devilish spirits,   80
You cannot but forbear to murther me.
This tongue hath parley'd unto foreign kings
For your behoof,—

   Cade. Tut! when struck'st thou one blow in the
    field?   84

   Say. Great men have reaching hands: oft have I
   struck
Those that I never saw, and struck them dead.

   Geo. O monstrous coward! what, to come
behind folks!   88

   Say. These cheeks are pale for watching for your
   good.

   Cade. Give him a box o' the ear, and that
will make 'em red again.

   Say. Long sitting, to determine poor men's causes, 92
Hath made me full of sickness and diseases.

   Cade. Ye shall have a hempen caudle then,
and the help of hatchet.

   Dick. Why dost thou quiver, man?   96

   Say. The palsy, and not fear, provokes me.

77 book: *i.e. learning*   85 reaching: *far-reaching*
94 hempen caudle: *hangman's noose*
95 help of hatchet: *i.e. cure by decapitation*

Cade. Nay, he nods at us; as who should say,
I'll be even with you: I'll see if his head will
stand steadier on a pole, or no. Take him away 100
and behead him.

Say. Tell me wherein have I offended most?
Have I affected wealth, or honour? speak.
Are my chests fill'd up with extorted gold?   104
Is my apparel sumptuous to behold?
Whom have I injur'd, that ye seek my death?
These hands are free from guiltless bloodshedding,
This breast from harbouring foul deceitful thoughts.
O! let me live.

Cade. [*Aside.*] I feel remorse in myself with
his words; but I'll bridle it: he shall die, an it
be but for pleading so well for his life. Away 112
with him! he has a familiar under his tongue;
he speaks not o' God's name. Go, take him
away, I say, and strike off his head presently;
and then break into his son-in-law's house, Sir 116
James Cromer, and strike off his head, and
bring them both upon two poles hither.

All. It shall be done.

Say. Ah, countrymen! if when you make your
prayers,   120
God should be so obdurate as yourselves,
How would it fare with your departed souls?
And therefore yet relent, and save my life.

Cade. Away with him! and do as I com- 124
mand ye. [*Exeunt some, with Lord Say.*] The
proudest peer in the realm shall not wear a
head on his shoulders, unless he pay me tribute;
there shall not a maid be married, but she shall 128

103 affected: *set my heart on*
107 guiltless bloodshedding: *shedding of guiltless blood*
113 familiar: *attendant demon*
                                                    114 o': *in*

pay to me her maidenhead, ere they have it;
men shall hold of me *in capite;* and we charge
and command that their wives be as free as
heart can wish or tongue can tell.　　　132

Dick. My lord, when shall we go to Cheapside and take up commodities upon our bills?

Cade. Marry, presently.

All. O! brave!　　　136

*Enter one with the heads [of Lord Say and Sir James
Cromer].*

Cade. But is not this braver? Let them kiss
one another, for they loved well when they were
alive. Now part them again, lest they consult
about the giving up of some more towns in 140
France. Soldiers, defer the spoil of the city
until night: for with these borne before us, instead of maces, will we ride through the streets;
and at every corner have them kiss. Away!　　　144

Exit [with his followers].

Scene Eight

[*The Same. Southwark*]

*Alarum and Retreat. Enter again Cade, and all his
rabblement.*

Cade. Up Fish Street! down St. Magnus'
corner! kill and knock down! throw them into
Thames!　　　*Sound a parley.*
What noise is this I hear? Dare any be so bold 4
to sound retreat or parley, when I command
them kill?

130 in capite: *by direct grant (with a pun)*
134 bills: *halberds (with pun on bills of credit)*　　　1 Fish Street; *cf. n.*

Enter Buckingham, and Old Clifford [with Forces].

Buck. Ay, here they be that dare and will disturb
    thee.
Know, Cade, we come ambassadors from the king   8
Unto the commons whom thou hast misled;
And here pronounce free pardon to them all
That will forsake thee and go home in peace.

Clif. What say ye, countrymen? will ye relent,   12
And yield to mercy, whilst 'tis offer'd you,
Or let a rebel lead you to your deaths?
Who loves the king, and will embrace his pardon,
Fling up his cap, and say 'God save his majesty!'   16
Who hateth him, and honours not his father,
Henry the Fifth, that made all France to quake,
Shake he his weapon at us, and pass by.

All. God save the king! God save the king!   20

Cade. What! Buckingham and Clifford, are
ye so brave? And you, base peasants, do ye
believe him? will you needs be hanged with your
pardons about your necks? Hath my sword 24
therefore broke through London Gates, that you
should leave me at the White Hart in Southwark? I thought ye would never have given out
these arms till you had recovered your ancient 28
freedom; but you are all recreants and dastards,
and delight to live in slavery to the nobility.
Let them break your backs with burthens, take
your houses over your heads, ravish your wives 32
and daughters before your faces: for me, I will
make shift for one, and so, God's curse light
upon you all!

All. We'll follow Cade, we'll follow Cade!   36

Clif. Is Cade the son of Henry the Fifth,

26 the White Hart; *cf. n.*   27 given out: *yielded up*

That thus you do exclaim you'll go with him?
Will he conduct you through the heart of France,
And make the meanest of you earls and dukes?   40
Alas! he hath no home, no place to fly to;
Nor knows he how to live but by the spoil,
Unless by robbing of your friends and us.
Were 't not a shame that, whilst you live at jar,   44
The fearful French, whom you late vanquished,
Should make a start o'er seas and vanquish you?
Methinks already in this civil broil
I see them lording it in London streets,   48
Crying *Villiago!* unto all they meet.
Better ten thousand base-born Cades miscarry,
Than you should stoop unto a Frenchman's mercy.
To France, to France! and get what you have lost;   52
Spare England, for it is your native coast.
Henry hath money, you are strong and manly;
God on our side, doubt not of victory.

All. A Clifford! a Clifford! we'll follow the   56
king and Clifford.

Cade. [*Aside.*] Was ever feather so lightly
blown to and fro as this multitude? The name of
Henry the Fifth hales them to an hundred mis-   60
chiefs, and makes them leave me desolate. I see
them lay their heads together to surprise me.
My sword make way for me, for here is no staying. In despite of the devils and hell, have   64
through the very middest of you! and heavens
and honour be witness, that no want of resolution
in me, but only my followers' base and ignominious treasons, makes me betake me to my heels.   68
                                        Exit.

Buck. What, is he fled? go some, and follow him;

And he that brings his head unto the king
Shall have a thousand crowns for his reward.

                              Exeunt some of them.

Follow me, soldiers: we'll devise a mean   72
To reconcile you all unto the king.   *Exeunt omnes.*

Scene Nine

[Kenilworth Castle]

*Sound Trumpets. Enter King, Queen, and Somerset
on the Terrace.*

  King. Was ever king that joy'd an earthly throne,
And could command no more content than I?
No sooner was I crept out of my cradle
But I was made a king at nine months old: 4
Was never subject long'd to be a king
As I do long and wish to be a subject.

       Enter Buckingham and Clifford.

  Buck. Health, and glad tidings, to your majesty!
  King. Why, Buckingham, is the traitor Cade sur-
      pris'd?   8
Or is he but retir'd to make him strong?

  Enter multitudes with halters about their necks.

  Clif. He's fled, my lord, and all his powers do yield;
And humbly thus, with halters on their necks,
Expect your highness' doom, of life, or death.   12
  King. Then, heaven, set ope thy everlasting gates,
To entertain my vows of thanks and praise!
Soldiers, this day have you redeem'd your lives,
And show'd how well you love your prince and
      country: 16

8 surpris'd: *taken prisoner*   14 entertain: *receive*

Continue still in this so good a mind,
And Henry, though he be infortunate,
Assure yourselves, will never be unkind:
And so, with thanks and pardon to you all,   20
I do dismiss you to your several countries.

    All. God save the king! God save the king!

Enter a Messenger.

    Mess. Please it your Grace to be advertised,
The Duke of York is newly come from Ireland;   24
And with a puissant and a mighty power
Of gallowglasses, and stout kerns,
Is marching hitherward in proud array;
And still proclaimeth, as he comes along,   28
His arms are only to remove from thee
The Duke of Somerset, whom he terms a traitor.

    King. Thus stands my state, 'twixt Cade and York
       distress'd;
Like to a ship, that, having scap'd a tempest,   32
Is straightway calm'd, and boarded with a pirate.
But now is Cade driven back, his men dispers'd;
And now is York in arms to second him.
I pray thee, Buckingham, go and meet him,   36
And ask him what's the reason of these arms.
Tell him I'll send Duke Edmund to the Tower;
And, Somerset, we will commit thee thither,
Until his army be dismiss'd from him.   40

    Som. My lord,
I'll yield myself to prison willingly,
Or unto death, to do my country good.

    King. In any case, be not too rough in terms;   44
For he is fierce and cannot brook hard language.

    Buck. I will, my lord; and doubt not so to deal

As all things shall redound unto your good.

    King. Come, wife, let's in, and learn to govern better; 48

For yet may England curse my wretched reign.

                        Flourish. Exeunt.

Scene Ten

[*Kent. Iden's Garden*]

Enter Cade

    Cade. Fie on ambitions! fie on myself, that have a sword, and yet am ready to famish! These five days have I hid me in these woods and durst not peep out, for all the country is laid 4 for me; but now I am so hungry, that if I might have a lease of my life for a thousand years I could stay no longer. Wherefore, on a brick wall have I climbed into this garden, to see if I 8 can eat grass, or pick a sallet another while, which is not amiss to cool a man's stomach this hot weather. And I think this word 'sallet' was born to do me good: for many a time, but 12 for a sallet, my brain-pan had been cleft with a brown bill; and many a time, when I have been dry, and bravely marching, it hath served me instead of a quart-pot to drink in; and now the 16 word 'sallet' must serve me to feed on.

Enter Iden.

    Iden. Lord! who would live turmoiled in the court,
And may enjoy such quiet walks as these?
This small inheritance my father left me 20

4 laid: *beset*   9 sallet: *salad of green herbs*
13 sallet: *light headpiece or helmet*

Contenteth me, and worth a monarchy.
I seek not to wax great by others' waning,
Or gather wealth I care not with what envy:
Sufficeth that I have maintains my state,   24
And sends the poor well pleased from my gate.

    Cade. [*Aside.*] Here's the lord of the soil
come to seize me for a stray, for entering his
fee-simple without leave. Ah, villain! thou wilt 28
betray me, and get a thousand crowns of the
king by carrying my head to him; but I'll make
thee eat iron like an ostrich, and swallow my
sword like a great pin, ere thou and I part.   32

    Iden. Why, rude companion, whatsoe'er thou be,
I know thee not; why then should I betray thee?
Is 't not enough to break into my garden,
And like a thief to come to rob my grounds,   36
Climbing my walls in spite of me the owner,
But thou wilt brave me with these saucy terms?

    Cade. Brave thee! ay, by the best blood that
ever was broached, and beard thee too. Look on 40
me well: I have eat no meat these five days;
yet, come thou and thy five men, and if I do
not leave you all as dead as a door-nail, I pray
God I may never eat grass more.   44

    Iden. Nay, it shall ne'er be said, while England
        stands,
That Alexander Iden, an esquire of Kent,
Took odds to combat a poor famish'd man.
Oppose thy steadfast-gazing eyes to mine,   48
See if thou canst out-face me with thy looks:
Set limb to limb, and thou art far the lesser;
Thy hand is but a finger to my fist;
Thy leg a stick compared with this truncheon;   52

21 and: *and so is*   24 Sufficeth that: *it is enough that what*
31 eat . . . ostrich; *cf. n.*   52 truncheon: *a thick staff* (*Iden's leg*)

My foot shall fight with all the strength thou hast;
And if mine arm be heaved in the air
Thy grave is digg'd already in the earth.
As for words, whose greatness answers words,   56
Let this my sword report what speech forbears.

    Cade. By my valour, the most complete
champion that ever I heard! Steel, if thou turn
the edge, or cut not out the burly-boned clown 60
in chines of beef ere thou sleep in thy sheath, I
beseech Jove on my knees, thou mayst be turned
to hobnails.

        Here they fight. [*Cade falls.*]

O, I am slain! Famine and no other hath slain 64
me: let ten thousand devils come against me, and
give me but the ten meals I have lost, and I'ld defy
them all. Wither, garden; and be henceforth a
burying-place to all that do dwell in this house, 68
because the unconquered soul of Cade is fled.

    Iden. Is 't Cade that I have slain, that monstrous
      traitor?

Sword, I will hallow thee for this thy deed,
And hang thee o'er my tomb when I am dead: 72
Ne'er shall this blood be wiped from thy point,
But thou shalt wear it as a herald's coat,
To emblaze the honour that thy master got.

    Cade. Iden, farewell; and be proud of thy 76
victory. Tell Kent from me, she hath lost her
best man, and exhort all the world to be
cowards; for I, that never feared any, am vanquished by famine, not by valour.   *Dies.* 80

    Iden. How much thou wrong'st me, heaven be my
      judge.

Die, damned wretch, the curse of her that bare thee!

56 *Cf. n.*

And as I thrust thy body in with my sword,
So wish I I might thrust thy soul to hell.   84
Hence will I drag thee headlong by the heels
Unto a dunghill which shall be thy grave,
And there cut off thy most ungracious head;
Which I will bear in triumph to the king,   88
Leaving thy trunk for crows to feed upon.

> *Exit* [*dragging out the body*].

ACT FIFTH

Scene One

[*Kent.   Fields between Dartford and Blackheath*]

*Enter York and his army of Irish, with drum and
colours.*

York. From Ireland thus comes York to claim his
right,
And pluck the crown from feeble Henry's head:
Ring, bells, aloud; burn, bonfires, clear and bright,
To entertain great England's lawful king.   4
Ah *sancta majestas,* who would not buy thee dear?
Let them obey that know not how to rule;
This hand was made to handle nought but gold:
I cannot give due action to my words,   8
Except a sword or sceptre balance it.
A sceptre shall it have, have I a soul,
On which I'll toss the flower-de-luce of France.

Enter Buckingham.

Whom have we here?   Buckingham, to disturb me? 12

83 thrust in: *pierce*   5 *Cf. n.*   8 action: *effect*
9 balance it: *add weight to my hand*   10 have I: *as sure as I have*
11 toss: *bear aloft*   flower-de-luce: *fleur de lys*

The king hath sent him, sure: I must dissemble.

   Buck. York, if thou meanest well, I greet thee well.

   York. Humphrey of Buckingham, I accept thy
     greeting.

Art thou a messenger, or come of pleasure?   16

   Buck. A messenger from Henry, our dread liege,

To know the reason of these arms in peace;

Or why thou,—being a subject as I am,—

Against thy oath and true allegiance sworn,   20

Should raise so great a power without his leave,

Or dare to bring thy force so near the court.

   York. [*Aside.*] Scarce can I speak, my choler is so
     great:

O! I could hew up rocks and fight with flint,   24

I am so angry at these abject terms;

And now, like Ajax Telamonius,

On sheep or oxen could I spend my fury.

I am far better born than is the king,   28

More like a king, more kingly in my thoughts;

But I must make fair weather yet awhile,

Till Henry be more weak, and I more strong.

[*Aloud.*] Buckingham, I prithee, pardon me   32

That I have given no answer all this while;

My mind was troubled with deep melancholy.

The cause why I have brought this army hither

Is to remove proud Somerset from the king,   36

Seditious to his Grace and to the state.

   Buck. That is too much presumption on thy part:

But if thy arms be to no other end,

The king hath yielded unto thy demand: 40

The Duke of Somerset is in the Tower.

   York. Upon thine honour, is he a prisoner?

   Buck. Upon mine honour, he is a prisoner.

---

15 Humphrey of Buckingham; *cf. n.*   26 Ajax Telamonius; *cf. n.*

York. Then, Buckingham, I do dismiss my powers. 44
Soldiers, I thank you all; disperse yourselves;
Meet me to-morrow in Saint George's Field,
You shall have pay, and everything you wish,
And let my sovereign, virtuous Henry,   48
Command my eldest son, nay, all my sons,
As pledges of my fealty and love;
I'll send them all as willing as I live:
Lands, goods, horse, armour, anything I have   52
Is his to use, so Somerset may die.

  Buck. York, I commend this kind submission:
We twain will go into his highness' tent.

Enter King and Attendants.

  King. Buckingham, doth York intend no harm to
    us,   56
That thus he marcheth with thee arm in arm?

  York. In all submission and humility
York doth present himself unto your highness.

  King. Then what intend these forces thou dost
    bring?   60

  York. To heave the traitor Somerset from hence,
And fight against that monstrous rebel, Cade,
Who since I heard to be discomfited.

Enter Iden, with Cade's head.

  Iden. If one so rude and of so mean condition   64
May pass into the presence of a king,
Lo! I present your Grace a traitor's head,
The head of Cade, whom I in combat slew.

  King. The head of Cade! Great God, how just art
    thou!   68
O! let me view his visage, being dead,
That living wrought me such exceeding trouble.

46 Saint George's Field; *cf. n.*   49 Command: *demand as hostage*

Tell me, my friend, art thou the man that slew him?

    Iden. I was, an 't like your majesty.   72

    King. How art thou call'd, and what is thy degree?

    Iden. Alexander Iden, that's my name;

A poor esquire of Kent, that loves his king.

    Buck. So please it you, my lord, 'twere not amiss 76

He were created knight for his good service.

    King. Iden, kneel down. [*He kneels.*] Rise up a knight.

We give thee for reward a thousand marks,

And will that thou henceforth attend on us.   80

    Iden. May Iden live to merit such a bounty,

And never live but true unto his liege!

Enter Queen and Somerset.

    King. See! Buckingham! Somerset comes with the queen:

Go, bid her hide him quickly from the duke.   84

    Queen. For thousand Yorks he shall not hide his head,

But boldly stand and front him to his face.

    York. How now! is Somerset at liberty?

Then, York, unloose thy long-imprison'd thoughts 88

And let thy tongue be equal with thy heart.

Shall I endure the sight of Somerset?

False king! why hast thou broken faith with me,

Knowing how hardly I can brook abuse?   92

King did I call thee? no, thou art not king;

Not fit to govern and rule multitudes,

Which dar'st not, no, nor canst not rule a traitor.

That head of thine doth not become a crown;   96

Thy hand is made to grasp a palmer's staff,

And not to grace an awful princely sceptre.

That gold must round engirt these brows of mine,

80 will: *command*

Whose smile and frown, like to Achilles' spear,   100
Is able with the change to kill and cure.
Here is a hand to hold a sceptre up,
And with the same to act controlling laws.
Give place: by heaven, thou shalt rule no more   104
O'er him whom heaven created for thy ruler.

Som. O monstrous traitor! I arrest thee, York,
Of capital treason 'gainst the king and crown.
Obey, audacious traitor; kneel for grace.   108

York. Wouldst have me kneel? first let me ask of
          these
If they can brook I bow a knee to man.
Sirrah, call in my sons to be my bail:
          [*Exit an Attendant.*]
I know ere they will have me go to ward,   112
They'll pawn their swords of my enfranchisement.

Queen. Call hither Clifford; bid him come amain,
To say if that the bastard boys of York
Shall be the surety for their traitor father.   116
          [*Exit Buckingham.*]

York. O blood-bespotted Neapolitan,
Outcast of Naples, England's bloody scourge!
The sons of York, thy betters in their birth,
Shall be their father's bail; and bane to those   120
That for my surety will refuse the boys!

Enter Edward and Richard.

See where they come: I'll warrant they'll make it good.

Enter Clifford [and his son].

Queen. And here comes Clifford, to deny their bail.

100 Achilles' spear; *cf. n.*   103 act: *put into effect*
109 these: *his followers*   112 ward: *custody*
113 of: *in behalf of*   enfranchisement: *freedom*
114 amain: *with speed*   117 Neapolitan; *cf. n.*

Clif. [*Kneeling.*] Health and all happiness to my
 lord the king!   124
   York. I thank thee, Clifford: say, what news with
      thee?
Nay, do not fright us with an angry look:
We are thy sovereign, Clifford, kneel again;
For thy mistaking so we pardon thee.   128
   Clif. This is my king, York, I do not mistake;
But thou mistak'st me much to think I do.
To Bedlam with him! is the man grown mad?
   King. Ay, Clifford; a bedlam and ambitious humour
Makes him oppose himself against his king.
   Clif. He is a traitor; let him to the Tower,
And chop away that factious pate of his.
   Queen. He is arrested, but will not obey: 136
His sons, he says, shall give their words for him.
   York. Will you not, sons?
   Edw. Ay, noble father, if our words will serve.
   Rich. And if words will not, then our weapons
      shall.   140
   Clif. Why, what a brood of traitors have we here!
   York. Look in a glass, and call thy image so:
I am thy king, and thou a false-heart traitor.
Call hither to the stake my two brave bears,   144
That with the very shaking of their chains
They may astonish these fell-lurking curs:
Bid Salisbury and Warwick come to me.

Enter the Earls of Warwick and Salisbury.

   Clif. Are these thy bears? we'll bait thy bears to
      death,   148
And manacle the bearard in their chains,

140 *Cf. n.*   144 two brave bears; *cf. n.*
146 fell-lurking: *watching to do mischief*
149 bearard: *bear-ward, keeper of bears*

If thou dar'st bring them to the baiting-place.

Rich. Oft have I seen a hot o'erweening cur
Run back and bite, because he was withheld;   152
Who, being suffer'd, with the bear's fell paw,
Hath clapp'd his tail between his legs, and cried:
And such a piece of service will you do,
If you oppose yourselves to match Lord Warwick. 156

Clif. Hence, heap of wrath, foul indigested lump,
As crooked in thy manners as thy shape!

York. Nay, we shall heat you thoroughly anon.

Clif. Take heed, lest by your heat you burn yourselves.   160

King. Why, Warwick, hath thy knee forgot to bow?
Old Salisbury, shame to thy silver hair,
Thou mad misleader of thy brain-sick son!
What! wilt thou on thy death-bed play the ruffian, 164
And seek for sorrow with thy spectacles?
O! where is faith? O, where is loyalty?
If it be banish'd from the frosty head,
Where shall it find a harbour in the earth?   168
Wilt thou go dig a grave to find out war,
And shame thine honourable age with blood?
Why art thou old, and want'st experience?
Or wherefore dost abuse it, if thou hast it?   172
For shame! in duty bend thy knee to me,
That bows unto the grave with mickle age.

Sal. My lord, I have consider'd with myself
The title of this most renowned duke;   176
And in my conscience do repute his Grace
The rightful heir to England's royal seat.

150 baiting-place: *bear-pit*
153 suffer'd: *allowed to have his way*   with: *at a blow of*
156 oppose yourselves: *venture*
157 indigested: *unformed, shapeless*
165 with . . . spectacles: *with careful scrutiny*
169 *Will you ensure your own death by promoting war?*
174 That: *i.e. thy knee*   mickle: *much*

    King. Hast thou not sworn allegiance unto me?

  Sal. I have.   180

    King. Canst thou dispense with heaven for such an
    oath?

  Sal. It is great sin to swear unto a sin,

But greater sin to keep a sinful oath.

Who can be bound by any solemn vow   184

To do a murderous deed, to rob a man,

To force a spotless virgin's chastity,

To reave the orphan of his patrimony,

To wring the widow from her custom'd right,   188

And have no other reason for this wrong

But that he was bound by a solemn oath?

    Queen. A subtle traitor needs no sophister.

    King. Call Buckingham, and bid him arm him-
    self.   192

    York. Call Buckingham, and all the friends thou
    hast,

I am resolv'd for death or dignity.

    Clif. The first I warrant thee, if dreams prove true.

    War. You were best to go to bed and dream again,

To keep thee from the tempest of the field.

    Clif. I am resolv'd to bear a greater storm

Than any thou canst conjure up to-day;

And that I'll write upon thy burgonet,   200

Might I but know thee by thy household badge.

    War. Now, by my father's badge, old Nevil's crest,

The rampant bear chain'd to the ragged staff,

This day I'll wear aloft my burgonet,—   204

---

181 dispense with: *get exemption from*   182 swear: *pledge oneself*
187 reave: *bereave*   188 custom'd: *sanctioned by custom*
191 sophister: *teacher of equivocation*
194 resolv'd for: *determined to win*
196 You . . . best: *it would be best for you*
200 burgonet: *helmet*
201 household badge: *distinguishing emblem of a family*
202, 203 *Cf. n.*   204 aloft: *on top of*

As on a mountain-top the cedar shows,
That keeps his leaves in spite of any storm,—
Even to affright thee with the view thereof.

Clif. And from thy burgonet I'll rend thy bear,   208
And tread it underfoot with all contempt,
Despite the bearard that protects the bear.

Y. Clif. And so to arms, victorious father,
To quell the rebels and their complices.   212

Rich. Fie! charity! for shame! speak not in spite,
For you shall sup with Jesu Christ to-night.

Y. Clif. Foul stigmatic, that's more than thou canst
   tell.

Rich. If not in heaven, you'll surely sup in hell.

Exeunt.

Scene Two

[Saint Albans]

[Alarums: Excursions.]   Enter Warwick.

War. Clifford of Cumberland, 'tis Warwick calls:
And if thou dost not hide thee from the bear,
Now, when the angry trumpet sounds alarum,
And dead men's cries do fill the empty air,   4
Clifford, I say, come forth, and fight with me!
Proud northern lord, Clifford of Cumberland,
Warwick is hoarse with calling thee to arms.

Enter York.

How now, my noble lord! what! all afoot?   8

York. The deadly-handed Clifford slew my steed;
But match to match I have encounter'd him,
And made a prey for carrion kites and crows

212 complices: *accomplices*
215 stigmatic: *one branded with deformity*   2 And if: *An if, if*

Even of the bonny beast he lov'd so well.   12

Enter Clifford.

War. Of one or both of us the time is come.

York. Hold, Warwick! seek thee out some other
chase,

For I myself must hunt this deer to death.

War. Then, nobly, York; 'tis for a crown thou
fight'st.   16

As I intend, Clifford, to thrive to-day,

It grieves my soul to leave thee unassail'd.   *Exit War.*

Clif. What seest thou in me, York? why dost thou
pause?

York. With thy brave bearing should I be in love, 20

But that thou art so fast mine enemy.

Clif. Nor should thy prowess want praise and
esteem,

But that 'tis shown ignobly and in treason.

York. So let it help me now against thy sword   24

As I in justice and true right express it.

Clif. My soul and body on the action both!

York. A dreadful lay! address thee instantly.

Clif. La fin couronne les œuvres.   28

[*They fight, and Clifford falls and dies.*]

York. Thus war hath given thee peace, for thou art
still.

Peace with his soul, heaven, if it be thy will!   *Exit.*

Enter Young Clifford.

Y. Clif. Shame and confusion! all is on the rout:

Fear frames disorder, and disorder wounds   32

Where it should guard.   O war! thou son of hell,

---

21 fast: *inalterably*

27 lay: *stake*   address thee: *prepare*   26 action: *result of combat*

28 La fin . . . œuvres: *'finis coronat opus,' the result proves the justice of the cause*

Whom angry heavens do make their minister,
Throw in the frozen bosoms of our part
Hot coals of vengeance!   Let no soldier fly: 36
He that is truly dedicate to war
Hath no self-love; nor he that loves himself
Hath not essentially, but by circumstance,
The name of valour.   [*Seeing his father's body.*]
              O, let the vile world end,   40
And the premised flames of the last day
Knit heaven and earth together;
Now let the general trumpet blow his blast,
Particularities and petty sounds   44
To cease!—Wast thou ordain'd, dear father,
To lose thy youth in peace, and to achieve
The silver livery of advised age,
And in thy reverence and thy chair-days thus   48
To die in ruffian battle?   Even at this sight
My heart is turn'd to stone: and while 'tis mine
It shall be stony.   York not our old men spares;
No more will I their babes: tears virginal   52
Shall be to me even as the dew to fire;
And beauty, that the tyrant oft reclaims,
Shall to my flaming wrath be oil and flax.
Henceforth I will not have to do with pity: 56
Meet I an infant of the house of York,
Into as many gobbets will I cut it
As wild Medea young Absyrtus did:
In cruelty will I seek out my fame.   60

35 part: *party, side*
39 not . . . circumstance: *not really but through accident*
41 premised: *sent before their time* (?), *foreordained* (?)
44 Particularities: *individual affairs*
45 cease: *put an end to*   47 advised: *experienced, cautious*
48 reverence: *state of dignity*   chair-days: *time of repose*
53 as . . . fire: *i.e. shall make the flame hotter*
54 that . . . reclaims: *which often subdues ferocity*
59 Medea . . . Absyrtus; *cf. n.*

Come, thou new ruin of old Clifford's house:

                                [Taking up the body.]

As did Æneas old Anchises bear,
So bear I thee upon my manly shoulders;
But then Æneas bare a living load,   64
Nothing so heavy as these woes of mine.   *[Exit.]*

        Enter Richard and Somerset to fight.
                [Somerset is killed.]

   Rich. So, lie thou there;
For underneath an alehouse' paltry sign,
The Castle in Saint Albans, Somerset   68
Hath made the wizard famous in his death.
Sword, hold thy temper; heart, be wrathful still:
Priests pray for enemies, but princes kill.   *[Exit.]*

Fight. Excursions. Enter King, Queen, and others.

   Queen. Away, my lord! you are slow: for shame,
     away!   72
   King. Can we outrun the heavens? good Margaret,
     stay.
   Queen. What are you made of? you'll nor fight nor
     fly:
Now is it manhood, wisdom, and defence
To give the enemy way, and to secure us   76
By what we can, which can no more but fly.

                              Alarum afar off.

If you be ta'en, we then should see the bottom
Of all our fortunes: but if we haply scape,
As well we may, if not through your neglect,   80

65 Nothing: *in no respect*
69 the wizard: *i.e. the Spirit (cf. I. iv. 38-40)*
74 nor . . . nor: *neither . . . nor*
76 secure us: *make ourselves safe*
77 which can: *we who can do*
                                   78, 79 *Cf. n.*
80 if . . . neglect: *if we do not fail through your negligence*

We shall to London get, where you are lov'd,
And where this breach now in our fortunes made
May readily be stopp'd.

Enter [Young] Clifford.

Clif. But that my heart's on future mischief set,   84
I would speak blasphemy ere bid you fly;
But fly you must: uncurable discomfit
Reigns in the hearts of all our present parts.
Away, for your relief! and we will live   88
To see their day and them our fortune give.
Away, my lord, away!   *Exeunt.*

Scene Three

[Field near Saint Albans]

Alarum.   Retreat.   Enter York, Richard, Warwick,
and Soldiers, with drum and colours.

York. Of Salisbury, who can report of him,
That winter lion, who in rage forgets
Aged contusions and all brush of time,
And, like a gallant in the brow of youth,   4
Repairs him with occasion? this happy day
Is not itself, nor have we won one foot,
If Salisbury be lost.
     Rich.   My noble father,
Three times to-day I holp him to his horse,   8
Three times bestrid him; thrice I led him off,
Persuaded him from any further act:

---

86 discomfit: *discouragement*
87 all . . . parts: *all of our party here*
89 their day: *a day of victory like theirs*   them . . . give: *impose on*
     them a misfortune like this of ours   2 winter: *aged*
3 brush: *wear and tear*   4 brow: *forefront*
5 Repairs . . . occasion: *grows more vigorous as he is called upon to
     exert himself*   9 bestrid: *stood over, to defend him when prostrate*

But still, where danger was, still there I met him;
And like rich hangings in a homely house,   1
So was his will in his old feeble body.
But, noble as he is, look where he comes.

Enter Salisbury.

Sal. Now, by my sword, well hast thou fought
 to-day;
By the mass, so did we all.   I thank you, Richard: 16
God knows how long it is I have to live;
And it hath pleas'd him that three times to-day
You have defended me from imminent death.
Well, lords, we have not got that which we have: 20
'Tis not enough our foes are this time fled,
Being opposites of such repairing nature.

 York. I know our safety is to follow them;
For, as I hear, the king is fled to London,   24
To call a present court of parliament:
Let us pursue him ere the writs go forth:—
What says Lord Warwick? shall we after them?

 War. After them! nay, before them, if we can.   28
Now, by my hand, lords, 'twas a glorious day:
Saint Albans battle, won by famous York,
Shall be eterniz'd in all age to come.
Sound, drums and trumpets, and to London all: 32
And more such days as these to us befall!   *Exeunt.*

11 still: *always*   20 got: *secured firmly*
22 opposites: *adversaries*   of . . . nature: *so endowed with means*
 of recovery   26 writs; *cf. n.*

FINIS.

NOTES

The Second Part of Henry the Sixth. The last word is written 'Sixt' in the early editions, that being the regular Elizabethan form of the numeral.

I. i. 58-63. *It is further agreed between them, etc.* Editors have not failed to observe that the wording of the document here differs from what Gloucester has just read, ll. 50 ff. Such inconsistency is very common in Shakespeare. Compare I. iv, lines 35 ff. and 67 ff. It is not necessary to explain that Gloucester's eyes were dim, or that his agitation prevented him from getting more than the general import of the passage. The author was writing for auditors, who would not compare the two texts.

I. i. 65. *We here create thee the first Duke of Suffolk.* The Earl of Suffolk was created Marquis, September 14, 1444, and was made Duke, June 2, 1448, three years after the coronation of Queen Margaret (May, 1445). The earlier dignity is the one which chronologically belongs in this scene; but the author is doubtless thinking of Holinshed's account of the later one: 'the marquesse of Suffolke, by great fauour of the king, & more desire of the queene, was erected to the title and dignitie of duke of Suffolke, which he a short time inioied.'

I. i. 68, 69. *till term of eighteen months Be full expir'd.* York is discharged for the term of the truce with the French king. Cf. line 42 above.

I. i. 120. *Anjou and Maine! myself did win them both.* An entirely unhistoric statement (found in the *Contention* version also). The earliest military service that Warwick saw was at the first battle of St. Albans, with which this play concludes (May 22, 1455). The present Earl of Warwick, the King-maker, is probably here confused with his father-in-law, from whom he derived his title. The earlier Earl, who died in 1439, appears in *The First Part of Henry VI* as a general on service in France. This is perhaps an indication that the authors of the *Contention* and of the *First Part* were not the same. (Actually the King-maker did not become Earl of Warwick till 1449. In the historical year of this scene, 1445, the earldom was held by the young son of the Earl who fought in France.)

I. i. 125. *For Suffolk's duke, may he be suffocate.* Poor puns are frequent in this play.

I. i. 134, 135. *That Suffolk should demand a whole fifteenth For costs and charges in transporting her.* A tax of one-fifteenth on personal property. The lines are suggested by Holinshed: 'for the fetching of hir, the marquesse of Suffolke demanded a whole fifteenth in open parliament.' In the concluding scene of the *First Part* (V. v. 92 f.), King Henry authorizes Suffolk to levy a greater tax:

> 'For your expenses and sufficient charge,
> Among the people gather up a tenth.'

I. i. 144, 145. *If I longer stay, We shall begin our ancient bickerings.* Allusion to the quarrels of Gloucester and the Cardinal in the *First Part.* This is one of the passages added by the reviser.

I. i. 153. *heir apparent to the English crown.* A misuse of the term, according to modern practice, for Gloucester was heir presumptive, not heir apparent; i.e. his right to succeed was contingent upon the chance that Henry would leave no lineal heir.

I. i. 155. *all the wealthy kingdoms of the west.* Perhaps an anachronistic allusion to the golden realms of Spanish America.

I. i. 166, 167. *Why should he then protect our sovereign, He being of age to govern of himself?* King

Henry was twenty-five years old at the time of Gloucester's death in 1447. Gloucester, however, had ceased to be Protector in name, or even in fact, long before. His formal Protectorship was annulled in 1429, when the king was crowned (at the age of seven). Thereafter Gloucester held no higher title than that of 'First Councillor.'

I. i. 181. *Pride went before, ambition follows him.* 'Pride' stands for the Cardinal, 'ambition' for Buckingham and Somerset.

I. i. 192, 193. *Thy deeds, thy plainness, and thy housekeeping Hath won the greatest favour of the commons.* Many modern editors alter 'hath' to 'have,' but Elizabethan English often prefers a logical to a grammatical agreement between subject and verb. 'Hath' may be explained as agreeing with the nearest of the three subjects, or with the aggregate idea of Warwick's character implied by all three. Frequently the lack of agreement is only apparent, not real (cf. note on I. iv. 77).

I. i. 195. *brother York, thy acts in Ireland.* Salisbury and York were brothers-in-law (see note on line 241 below). York's 'acts in Ireland' were not performed till later than the historical date of this scene (1445). His highly successful administration of Ireland occurred in 1448-1450. Compare the note on III. i. 318.

I. i. 235, 236. *As did the fatal brand Althæa burnt Unto the prince's heart of Calydon.* The heart of the prince of Calydon (Meleager) succumbed to death when his mother in anger burned the piece of firewood ('brand'), which the Fates had prophesied would measure his length of life. This passage, like many others of a flowery and rhetorical nature, is not found in the original (*Contention*) version, and was presumably added by Shakespeare. It has been noted that the myth is here correctly reproduced from Ovid, whereas in *2 Henry IV* (II. ii. 96-100) the poet seems to retain only a confused recollection of it.

I. i. 241. *And therefore I will take the Nevils' parts.* York's wife was Cecily, youngest sister of Richard Nevil, Earl of Salisbury, and aunt of Warwick. Actually it was the Nevils who took York's part. (Compare note on I. iii. 75-77.)

I. ii. 9. *grovel on thy face.* Solicit supernatural aid. Compare I. iv. 13, 14.

I. ii. 38. *in that chair where kings and queens are crown'd.* The 'chair of Scone' at Westminster. The stone of destiny which formed its seat was brought by Edward I from Scotland in 1296.

I. ii. 68. *Sir John.* Not a title of knighthood, but a common form of address for priests. In such cases it signifies no more than 'Dominie.'

I. ii. 71. *I am but Grace.* 'Your Grace' being the proper salutation for a Duchess. In Shakespeare, however, it is frequently used in addressing kings and queens, as in the next scene of this play, line 70.

I. iii. 18-22. *Mine is, an't please your Grace, against John Goodman, my Lord Cardinal's man, for keeping my house, and lands, my wife and all, from me. Suf. Thy wife too! that is some wrong indeed.* This passage, which is considerably developed from its source in the *Contention,* shows in its revised form a strong similarity to the opening scene of the play of *Sir Thomas More,* in which Shakespeare is thought to have had a part. Some of the Jack Cade scenes of the present play likewise betray a close affinity to *Sir Thomas More.*

I. iii. 23-25. *Against the Duke of Suffolk, for enclosing the commons of Melford.* Long Melford is a town in the county of Suffolk. The form of oppression represented by the appropriation and fencing in by wealthy citizens of common land was frequent in the sixteenth century. Some of the latest records of

Shakespeare's life deal with his attitude toward the project of enclosing the common at Welcombe near Stratford. His kinsman, Thomas Greene, wrote as follows, November 17, 1614: 'My cosen Shakspear comyng yesterdy to town, I went to see him how he did. He told me that they assured him they ment to inclose no further than to Gospell Bush, and so upp straight (leavyng out part of the Dyngles to the ffield) to the gate in Clopton hedg, and take in Salisburyes peece; and that they mean in Aprill to survey the land, and then to gyve satisfaccion, and not before; and he and Mr. Hall [Shakespeare's son-in-law] say they think ther will be nothyng done at all.' On September 1, 1615, Greene wrote in his Diary: 'Mr. Shakspeare told Mr. J. Greene that I was not able to beare the enclosing of Welcombe.'

I. iii. 63. *canoniz'd*. The accent is on the second syllable, as regularly in Shakespeare.

I. iii. 75-77. *And he of these that can do most of all Cannot do more in England than the Nevils: Salisbury and Warwick are no simple peers*. These lines are not found in the *Contention* version, and may be fairly credited to Shakespeare's Warwickshire memories of the Nevils. This noble family—'of all the great houses of mediaeval England . . . incontestibly the toughest and the most prolific' (Oman)—originated in the north, about Raby Castle near Durham. The first earldom they acquired was that of Westmoreland, bestowed by Richard II upon Sir Ralph Nevil in 1397. The latter is the Earl of Westmoreland who appears in Shakespeare's plays of *Henry IV* and *Henry V*. He married, as his second wife, a daughter of John of Gaunt, sister of the Cardinal Beaufort of the present play. Salisbury was their son and Warwick their grandson.

I. iii. 105. *Or Somerset or York, all's one to me.* Holinshed records that at the expiration of York's

term as Regent of France (in 1446), 'he returned
home, and was ioifullie receiued of the king with
thanks for his good seruice, as he had full well de-
serued in time of that his gouernement: and, further,
that now, when a new regent was to be chosen and sent
ouer, to abide vpon safegard of the countries beyond
the seas as yet subiect to the English dominion, the
said duke of Yorke was eftsoones (as a man most meet
to supplie that roome) appointed to go ouer againe, as
regent of France, with all his former allowances.

'But the duke of Summerset, still maligning the
duke of Yorkes aduancement, as he had sought to
hinder his dispatch at the first when he was sent ouer
to be regent, (as before yee haue heard,) he likewise
now wrought so, that the king reuoked his grant made
to the duke of Yorke for enioieng of that office the
terme of other fiue yeeres, and, with helpe of William
marquesse of Suffolke, obteined that grant for him-
selfe.' In connection with the latter part of this ex-
tract, see lines 162 ff.

I. iii. 121, 122. *If he be old enough, what needs
your Grace To be protector of his excellence?* As
before noted, this title had long since lapsed. Observe
Gloucester's reply and see note on I. i. 166, 167.

I. iii. 128. *The Dauphin hath prevail'd beyond the
seas.* Since the sovereignty of the French king,
Charles VII, was not acknowledged by the English,
they continued to designate him by the title ('Dolphin'
in Elizabethan spelling) he had borne during his
father's lifetime. The particular victories for the
Dauphin here referred to are probably those obtained
in 1443-1444 over John, the first Duke of Somerset,
brother of the Duke who appears in this scene. By
the influence of his uncle, Cardinal Beaufort, the first
duke was appointed, on March 30, 1443, 'Captain-
General of all France and Guienne.' After a campaign of utter disaster, he returned to England and

died in May, 1444. His failure was in a way a vin-
dication, not a disgrace, for Gloucester.

I. iii. 133. *Thy sumptuous buildings.* The Duke
occupied Greenwich Palace, which was greatly enlarged and improved by his Renaissance taste. In
Shakespeare's time it was a favorite residence of
Queen Elizabeth and King James.

I. iii. 144, 145. *Could I come near your beauty
with my nails, I'd set my ten commandments in your
face.* This undignified scene is historically impossible.
The Queen and Duchess never met, for the humiliation
and banishment of the latter, depicted in Act II, scene
iv, occurred in 1441, four years before Margaret came
to England.

I. iii. 174, 175. *Last time I danc'd attendance on
his will Till Paris was besieg'd, famish'd, and lost.*
The loss of Paris occurred in 1437, seven years before
the present Duke of Somerset came to his title. York,
however, is probably alluding to a scene in the *First
Part* (IV. iii. 9-11), where he complains of 'that villain Somerset,

> That thus delays my promised supply
> Of horsemen that were levied for this siege.'

This is in connection with the siege of Bordeaux and
last campaign of Talbot, 1453 (historically long after
the date of the present scene). These lines have again
been added by the reviser. Compare note on I. i. 144,
145.

I. iii. 215, 216. These lines are not in the Folio.
They have been introduced from the *Contention* version because Somerset's reply (line 217) seems to
presuppose them.

I. iv. 59. *A pretty plot, well chosen to build upon!*
There is a quibble on 'plot': a plot of ground and a
stratagem.

I. iv. 64, 65. *Why, this is just, 'Aio te, Æacida,
Romanos vincere posse.'* The cryptic answer about the

Duke of York and Henry, just quoted, is as ambiguous as the famous response given by the oracle to Pyrrhus, King of Epirus, which may be interpreted either, 'I say that you, descendant of Æacus, can conquer the Romans,' or 'I say that the Romans can conquer you.'

I. iv. 77. *Thither goes these news as fast as horse can carry them.* An example of Shakespeare's frequent use of an apparently singular verb with a plural subject. Compare note on I. i. 192, 193. The irregularity is usually to be explained by the fact that, while Shakespeare ordinarily used the midland verbal inflections which correspond with those of modern English, he was also familiar with the northern inflection, in which the present plural ends in 's,' and with the southern, in which it ends in 'eth.' Modern editors generally normalize the dialectal forms, except where rhyme or metre requires their retention. Other instances in which the Folio reading deviates from modern usage are the following: 'humours fits not' (I. i. 248), 'My troublous dreams this night doth make me sad' (I. ii. 22), 'What plain proceedings is more plain' (II. ii. 53), 'count them happy that enjoys the sun' (II. iv. 39), 'these dread curses . . . recoil, And turns the force of them upon thyself' (III. ii. 332), 'the traitors hateth thee' (IV. iv. 43), 'Let them obey that knows not how to rule' (V. i. 6), 'what intends these forces' (V. i. 60), 'thou mistakes me much' (V. i. 130).

II. i. 4. *old Joan had not gone out.* Old Joan (a hawk) would not have flown against such a wind.

II. i. 24. *Tantæne animis cœlestibus iræ?* A quotation from the first book of the Æneid (line 11): 'Are such furies possible to heavenly minds?'

II. i. 26. *With such holiness can you do it?* 'Holy as you seem to be, can you hide your malice?' Or perhaps, 'can you be so hot?'

II. i. 46-48. The Folio gives these three speeches

as one, spoken by Gloucester. Theobald made the change.

II. i. 63. *Saint Alban's shrine.* The town and abbey of St. Albans, twenty-two miles north of London, are named after the first Christian martyr in Britain, Saint Alban, who was put to death there, A. D. 304. The sham miracle is narrated by Sir Thomas More on the authority of his father. It was copied from More into Grafton's Chronicle, but not into those of Halle and Holinshed.

II. i. 91. *who said, 'Simon, come.'* Theobald has been generally followed in emending Simon to Simpcox, but the latter is merely a derivative of Simon, through Sim-cock (Simon boy). It is more in keeping with the saint's dignity to employ the Biblical name in its purity.

II. ii. 39-42. *This Edmund, in the reign of Bolingbroke, As I have read, laid claim unto the crown; And but for Owen Glendower, had been king, Who kept him in captivity till he died.* Here, as in *1 Henry IV,* I. iii. 145, and in *1 Henry VI,* II. v., the name Edmund Mortimer causes confusion. The Edmund Mortimer (5th Earl of March), who figured in the reign of Bolingbroke as heir to the throne, was (as York says in lines 43, 44) York's mother's brother. He did not die either in captivity to Glendower, as here stated, or in the Tower of London, as *1 Henry VI* represents. The Edmund Mortimer captured by Glendower was uncle of the other Edmund, being younger brother to Roger, fourth Earl of March. The erroneous statement that Glendower 'kept him in captivity till he died,' which contradicts Shakespeare's treatment of the situation in *1 Henry IV,* seems due to a further confusion of Sir Edmund Mortimer with another prisoner of Glendower, Lord Grey of Ruthin, whom the chroniclers report to have been kept a captive till his death. The *Contention* version of this scene gives

a quite different and even more garbled account o
these facts.

II. iii. 4. *Such as by God's book are adjudg'd t
death.* Cf. Exodus 22. 18: 'Thou shalt not suffer
witch to live'; and Leviticus 20. 6: 'And the soul tha
turneth after such as have familiar spirits, and afte
wizards . . . I will even set my face against that soul
and will cut him off from among his people.'

II. iii. 7, 8. *The witch in Smithfield shall b
burnt to ashes, And you three shall be strangled o
the gallows.* Holinshed's account is as follows: 'Mar
gerie Iordeine was burnt in Smithfield, and Roge
Bolinbrooke was drawne to Tiburne, and hanged an
quartered; taking vpon his death that there was neue
anie such thing by them imagined. Iohn Hun had hi
pardon, and Southwell died in the Tower the nigh
before his execution.' These lines dealing with the
punishment of the Duchess's accomplices are not foun
in the *Contention* version. Holinshed's statement that
Hun, or Hume, 'had his pardon' may have prompted
the suggestion in I. ii. 88 ff. that he betrayed the
Duchess's plot.

II. iii. 13. *With Sir John Stanley, in the Isle of
Man.* The dramatist appears here to be following
Halle's (or Grafton's) Chronicle. Holinshed gives
the name correctly as Sir Thomas Stanley. The error
is found in the *Contention* version (e.g., in lines corre-
sponding to II. iv. 78, 80, 85), and is not an evidence
that Shakespeare himself forsook his favorite Holinshed for Halle. (The present line is not in the *Contention.*)

II. iii. 46. *Thus Eleanor's pride dies in her youngest days.* Some editors take 'her' as referring to
'pride,' but the Duchess's pride is nowhere represented
as a newly acquired characteristic. Probably 'youngest' should be understood, like the Latin *novissimi*, as
latest, most recent, in which case the meaning is that
Eleanor's pride, so long maintained, dies at last.

II. iii. 97, 98. *I confess, I confess treason.* Holinshed makes it clear that the armorer 'was slaine without
guilt,'—as a result of intoxication and not of his un-
righteous cause.   Peter, on the other hand, was a false
servant who 'liued not long vnpunished; for being con-
uict of felonie in court of assise, he was iudged to be
hanged, and so was, at Tiburne.'   But it was the
design of the author of the *Contention*, whom the reviser here follows closely, to emphasize from the start
the treasonable purposes of York.

II. iv. 70-72.   *I summon your Grace to his
majesty's parliament, holden at Bury the first of this
next month.*   The three days' penance imposed on the
Duchess were November 13, 15, 17, 1441.   The Parliament at Bury St. Edmunds opened on February 10,
1447.   Gloucester arrived on the 18th and died on the
23d.

III. i. 1, 2.   *I muse my Lord of Gloucester is not
come: 'Tis not his wont to be the hindmost man.*   The
parliament had been in session for a week when
Gloucester arrived.   See previous note.

III. i. 9-12.   *We know the time since he was mild
and affable, And if we did but glance a far-off look,
Immediately he was upon his knee, That all the court
admir'd him for submission.*   This seems not to have
been true of Gloucester, who was of an obstinate dis-
position.   The lines are in the rhetorical style that the
reviser of this play particularly affects.   They are
evolved from a slight hint in the *Contention:*

> 'The time hath bene, but now that time is past,
>   That none so humble as Duke Humphrey was.'

III. i. 58, 59.   *Did he not, contrary to form of law,
Devise strange deaths for small offences done?*   'He
was accused, it is said, of malpractices during his Pro-
tectorate, especially of having caused men adjudged
to die to be put to other execution than the law of the

land allowed.' (Vickers, *Humphrey Duke of Glouces-ter*, p. 290.) The charge is found in the chroniclers, and has been suggested earlier in the play (I. iii. 135 f.).

III. i. 83-85. *Welcome, Lord Somerset. What news from France?* Som. *That all your interest in those territories Is utterly bereft you: all is lost.* This reports correctly Somerset's disastrous manage-ment of affairs in France from the time of his viola-tion of the truce in March, 1449, till his return to England in October, 1450. The events alluded to are about three years later than Gloucester's death, and about three years earlier than the death of Talbot (July, 1453), which is depicted in the *First Part*.

III. i. 87, 88. *Cold news for me; for I had hope of France, As firmly as I hope for fertile England.* These lines are repeated from I. i. 238, 239. Holinshed reports that Somerset's ignominious conduct in France 'kindled so great a rancor in the duke's [York's] heart and stomach, that he neuer left persecuting the duke of Summerset, vntill he had brought him to his fatall end and confusion.' In fact, York seems, however, not to have been the persecutor.

III. i. 97. *I do arrest thee of high treason here.* The circumstances of Gloucester's arrival in Bury and his arrest are given by Vickers, *op. cit.*, p. 292 f.: 'It was eleven o'clock in the morning when Gloucester rode into the city by the south gate, and passing through the "horsemarket," turned to his left into the Northgate Ward. Here he passed through a mean street, and as he rode along, he asked a passerby, by what name the alley was known. "Forsoothe, my Lord, hit is called the Dede [dead] Lane," came the answer. Then the inborn superstition of "the Good Duke" asserted itself; so with an old prophecy he had read ringing in his ears, and a word of pious resignation on his lips, he rode on to the "North Spytyll" outside the Northgate, otherwise called

"Seynt Salvatoures," where he was to lodge. Having eaten his dinner, a deputation came to wait upon him, consisting of the Duke of Buckingham, the Marquis of Dorset, the Earl of Salisbury, Lord Sudley, and Viscount Beaumont. The last in his capacity of High Constable placed the Duke under arrest by the King's command.'

III. i. 158-160. *And dogged York, that reaches at the moon, Whose overweening arm I have pluck'd back, By false accuse doth level at my life.* 'On the other hand, the Duke of York had come to the front as the opponent of the Beauforts and as a follower of Duke Humphrey, though he never came anywhere near to supplanting the latter as leader of the opposition to the existing state of government.' (Vickers, *op. cit.,* p. 307) 'To the majority of the English people York passed not as a disturber of the peace, but as a wronged and injured man, goaded into resistance by the machinations of the Court party. In one aspect he was regarded as a great lord of the royal blood excluded from his rightful place at the Council board, and even kept out of the country, by his enemies who had the King's ear. In another he was regarded as the leader and mouthpiece of the Opposition of the day, of the old and popular war-party which inherited the traditions of Henry the Fifth and Humphrey of Gloucester.' (Oman, *Warwick*, p. 42.) Holinshed and other chroniclers had pointed out that the removal of Gloucester left King Henry exposed to attack by the House of York; but it was the author of the *Contention* (closely followed in the lines above) who dramatized the Duke of York as a treacherous self-seeker, held in check by the good Duke Humphrey. The conception, while unfair to York, gave force and unity to the play.

III. i. 308. *And in the number thee, that wishest shame.* An allusion to the motto: '*Honi soit qui mal y pense.*'

III. i. 318. *Then, noble York, take thou this task in hand.* These lines introduce York's Lieutenancy in Ireland (1448-1450), which in the first scene of the play is alluded to as already past. See note on I. i. 195.

III. i. 331, 332. *Now, York, or never, steel thy fearful thoughts, And change misdoubt to resolution.* In the original (*Contention*) version these lines have a very different spirit:

> 'Now, York, bethink thyself and rouse thee vp,
> Take time whilst it is offered thee so fair.'

The speech as a whole, which has been expanded from twenty-four to fifty-three lines, is a very good example of the change Shakespeare's revision has wrought in York's character. The fearless, positive, and unscrupulous figure of the *Contention* is in the present play half concealed by an addition of sentimental, imaginative, and irresolute fancy.

III. i. 356-359. *I have seduc'd a headstrong Kentishman, John Cade of Ashford, To make commotion, as full well he can, Under the title of John Mortimer.* 'A certeine yoong man, of a goodlie stature and right pregnant of wit, was intised to take vpon him the name of Iohn Mortimer, coosine to the duke of Yorke; (although his name was Iohn Cade, or, of some, Iohn Mend-all, an Irishman, as *Polychronicon* saith).' (Holinshed.) The chroniclers do not assert that York was privy to Cade's rebellion. Lines 360-370, reciting Cade's performances in Ireland under the eye of York, are all new with the reviser of the play. They were probably inspired by Holinshed's remark that some authorities called Cade an Irishman.

III. ii. 14. S. d. In the Folio text Suffolk enters with the King, Queen, and the rest, having gone out previously with the Murderers. Thus a new scene should properly begin at this point; and this would be logical since Gloucester's death took place at a

dging at some distance from the king's court.
ditors have, however, preferred to retain the Quarto
Contention) arrangement, by which the Murderers
o out alone. 'Then enter the King and Queene' and
l the rest except Suffolk, who is at once directly ad-
ressed by the King: 'My Lord of Suffolk, go call our
ncle Gloster.'

III. ii. 26. *Meg.* In the Folio the word is 'Nell.'
o in lines 79, 100, and 120 'Elinor' (or 'Elianor')
ppears instead of the 'Margaret' which modern edi-
rs have substituted. None of the lines in question
ccur in the *Contention* version. They are to be
scribed to a slip of the reviser's pen, induced, of
ourse, by his familiarity with 'Nell' and 'Eleanor'
s applied to the Duchess of Gloucester in earlier
cenes. The mistake is of a sort more easily committed
y a reviser, applying patches throughout the play,
han by an author who thought in terms of the scene
s a whole.

III. ii. 60, 61. *heart-offending groans Or blood-
onsuming sighs.* Shakespeare is fond of the old idea
hat every sigh costs the heart a drop of blood. The
otion is here given in double form and then repeated
a line 63: 'blood-drinking sighs.' In the *Third Part,*
V. iv. 22, we have 'blood-sucking sighs.' Compare
l *Midsummer-Night's Dream,* III. ii. 97: 'with sighs
f love, that costs the fresh blood dear.'

III. ii. 76. *What! art thou, like the adder, waxen
eaf?* A common allusion which goes back to Psalm
8. 4, 5: 'they are like the deaf adder that stoppeth
er ear; Which will not hearken to the voice of
harmers, charming never so wisely.' Cf. Shake-
peare's 112th Sonnet, lines 10, 11: 'my adder's sense
o critic and to flatterer stopped are.'

III. ii. 116-118. *as Ascanius did, When he to
adding Dido would unfold His father's acts, com-
enc'd in burning Troy!* The allusion is new with
he reviser, and like many of Shakespeare's classical

references is not minutely accurate. It was Æne
himself who told Dido of his acts, and Ascanius,
son, was impersonated on that occasion by Cupid.

III. ii. 134, 135. *Stay, Salisbury, With the ru*
multitude till I return. Warwick speaks through t
door to his father, who does not enter the stage.

III. ii. 310. *Would curses kill, as doth the ma*
drake's groan. The mandrake, or mandragora, was
poisonous plant with narcotic properties. Its fork
root was supposed to resemble the human figure, a
to utter a cry when pulled from the ground whi
would kill or drive mad those who heard it. For t
latter penalty, cf. *Romeo and Juliet,* IV. iii. 48 f.

'And shrieks like mandrakes' torn out of the earth,
   That living mortals, hearing them, run mad.'

III. ii. 344, 345. *That thou might'st think up*
these by the seal, Through whom a thousand sighs a
breath'd for thee. As often in cases of difficult synta
Samuel Johnson's paraphrase has been found the mo
accurate: 'That by the impression of my kiss forev
remaining on thy hand thou mightest think on tho
lips through which a thousand sighs will be breathe
for thee.' 'These' in line 344 is the antecedent
'whom' and refers to Margaret's lips. The elabora
and 'precious' style which the reviser affects is we
illustrated when lines 343–345 are contrasted with th
plain language of the *Contention* version:

'Oh let this kisse be printed in thy hand,
   That when thou seest it, thou maist thinke on me.'

III. ii. 369. *Cardinal Beaufort is at point of deat*
Beaufort's death occurred on April 11, 1447, six week
after that of Gloucester, and three years before th
banishment of Suffolk (March 17, 1450). The un
favorable character of Beaufort which the dramatist
derived from the Tudor chroniclers is not historicall
justified. The aged cardinal's death seems in pai

icular to have been peaceful and dignified. See L. B.
Radford's judicial and sympathetic biography (*Henry
Beaufort, Bishop, Chancellor, Cardinal*, 1908).

III. ii. 393. *its lips.* One of the very rare instances
of the possessive *its* in Shakespeare. The correspond-
ing line of the *Contention* has 'his lips'; the Folio 'it's
lips.'

IV. i. 1-7. *The gaudy, blabbing, and remorseful
day Is crept into the bosom of the sea, And now loud-
howling wolves arouse the jades,* etc. 'These obvi-
ously additional lines, inartistically joined to the scene
by the word "Therefore" [line 8] bear impress of
Shakespeare's earliest Marlovian style, or rather
Peeleian, but vastly more powerful and more musical.'
(Hart.) The *Contention* version opens very simply
with the equivalent of line 8: 'Bring forward these
prisoners that scorn'd to yeeld.'

IV. i. 9. *whilst our pinnace anchors in the Downs.*
The Downs are a roadstead off the east coast of Kent,
protected by Goodwin Sands (which are mentioned
in *The Merchant of Venice*, III. i. 4). This reference
to the Downs is not in the *Contention* version. From
King Lear it would seem that Shakespeare must have
had some personal knowledge of the coast of Kent.

IV. i. 11. *Or with their blood stain this discolour'd
shore.* 'Discolour'd' is used 'proleptically': stain this
shore, which will then be discolored by their blood.

IV. i. 29. *Look on my George; I am a gentleman.*
An image of Saint George in gold was worn by
Knights of the Garter.

IV. i. 35. *And told me that by Water I should die.*
Compare I. iv. 36. The 'l' in Walter was silent, as in
the abbreviated form 'Wat.'

IV. i. 48-50. The Folio text of these lines is evidently corrupt, and has been corrected by comparison
with the *Contention*. The Folio omits line 48 and
gives line 50 as part of the Lieutenant's speech, making

Suffolk's answer begin with line 51. (For 'lowly' th
Folio reads 'lowsie.')

IV. i. 50. *King Henry's blood.* Suffolk had onl
a vague claim to kinship with the king. Our chie
interest in his family connection rests in the circum
stance that his wife, Alice Chaucer, appears to hav
been a granddaughter of the poet.

IV. i. 54. *my foot-cloth mule.* A mule capar
soned with an elaborate cloth of state, reaching t
the ground. Mules were highly regarded as mount.

IV. i. 84. *ambitious Sylla.* Lucius Cornelius Sull
or Sylla (ca. 138-78 B. C.), enemy of Marius an
author of the first great proscription or legalize
massacre in Roman history. He figures in Lodge'
play, *The Wounds of Civil War* (printed, 1594).

IV. i. 98. *Advance our half-fac'd sun, striving t
shine.* 'Edward III bare for his device the rays o
the sun dispersing themselves out of a cloud
(Camden.) The defeat of Warwick at Barnet wa
due to confusion of the badge of his supporter Oxfor
with the 'sun with rays' borne by Edward IV. 'Ox
ford's men, whose banners and armour bore the Ra
diant Star of the De Veres, were mistaken by thei
comrades for a flanking column of Yorkists. In th
mist their badge had been taken for the Sun wit
Rays, which was King Edward's cognisance.' (Oman
Warwick, p. 232.)

IV. i. 108. *Bargulus, the strong Illyrian pirate*
In the *Contention* the passage reads: 'mightie Abradas
The great Masadonian Pyrate,' a borrowing appar
ently from Greene, who wrote in his *Penelope's Web*
'Abradas the great Macedonian Pirat thought euer
one had a letter of mart that bare sayles in the Ocean
In his *Menaphon* Greene repeated the sentence verba
tim. Nothing further has been discovered concernin
Abradas. Bargulus is substituted in the Folio versio
of the play from Cicero's *De Officiis*, bk. ii, ch. 11
'Bargulus [properly Bardylis] Illyricus latro . .

magnas opes habuit.' Nicholas Grimald's translation of the *De Officiis* (1556) renders the phrase, 'Bargulus, that Illyrian robber.'

IV. i. 117. *Pene gelidus timor occupat artus.* 'Cold fear almost seizes my joints.' The Folio gives the first word as 'Pine,' which most editors omit as meaningless. Theobald interpreted it as 'pœnæ,' (fear) of punishment, and Malone as 'pene,' almost.

IV. i. 127. *let my head . . . sooner dance upon a bloody pole.* 'There is, indeed, one detail in the drama of the period which may be regarded as symbolical of the whole dramatic tendency of the time, namely, the swinging about of a human head, cut from its body, on the stage. This cut-off head was a stage-property that had survived from the time of the mystery-plays, when it was meant to represent the head of the unfortunate John the Baptist at the gruesome crowning point of the dance of Salome. It survived in several specimens, a favourite stage-property, in the popular theatre, certain, as we may presume, at every appearance of drawing the ironical applause of experienced theatre-goers, and probably known to the actors, whose sense of the comic was at all times keen, by some droll nickname now forgotten. In the three parts of the old drama of *Henry VI* this head appears at different times. Queen Margaret (*2 Henry VI*, IV. iv.) presses it to her bosom as the head of her dead lover, Suffolk. A few scenes later it appears in duplicate and with a different signification, again further on (V. i.) as the head of the rebel Cade.' (Schücking, *Character Problems in Shakespeare's Plays*, 1922, p. 19 f.)

IV. i. 137. *savage islanders.* Pompey was slain in Egypt, 48 B. C., not by savage islanders, but by Egyptians and renegade soldiers of his own. The error is not found in the *Contention*. It is a coincidence that in Chapman's *Tragedy of Cæsar and Pompey* (printed 1631) Pompey is murdered on the island of Lesbos.

IV. ii. 86, 87. *The first thing we do, let's kill all the lawyers.* The proposal to kill lawyers seems to have been a feature, not of Cade's rebellion, but of the earlier one led by Wat Tyler in 1381.

IV. ii. 111, 112. *They use to write it on the top of letters.* Emmanuel ('God with us') was placed as a pious sentiment at the head of letters and other documents.

IV. iii. 6-8. *the Lent shall be as long again as it is; and thou shalt have a licence to kill for a hundred lacking one.* The eating of flesh during Lent was forbidden in Elizabeth's reign, and killing of beasts at that time was permitted only by special license to provide for invalids (supposedly) unable to dispense with flesh. A license to kill for ninety-nine a week during a doubled Lent would thus constitute a valuable monopoly. 'For' in line 8 may mean 'at the rate of,' allowing Dick to slaughter ninety-nine beasts a week.

IV. vii. 23. *the Lord Say, which sold the towns in France.* Lord Say had been associated with Suffolk in the cession of Anjou and Maine.

IV. vii. 24. *he that made us pay one-and-twenty fifteens.* Twenty-one fifteens is a humorous exaggeration. A frequent mode of raising revenue to cover unusual expenditures of the government was to impose a tax of one-fifteenth (sometimes one-tenth) on personal property. Compare note on I. i. 134. One of Cade's actual demands was 'that neither fifteens should hereafter be demanded, nor once anie impositions or taxes be spoken of.'

IV. vii. 39. *the score and the tally.* Tallies were the two halves of a stick, split and divided between creditor and debtor. Scores were the notches on the tallies which served to certify the transactions.

IV. vii. 39, 40. *thou hast caused printing to be used.* An anachronism, since the first book printed in England was not produced till 1477. (Cade's rebellion

was in 1450, the outbreak following Suffolk's death
by two months.)

IV. vii. 55, 56. *when honester men than thou go in
their hose and doublets.* Hose and doublet were the
indispensable articles of dress, covering the lower and
upper parts of the body respectively. The cloak was
worn over hose and doublet by the well-to-do. For
the horse's 'cloak' or foot-cloth cf. note on IV. i. 54.

IV. vii. 65, 66. *Kent, in the Commentaries Cæsar
writ, Is term'd the civil'st place of all this isle.* The
wording, which is almost the same in the *Contention,*
is probably borrowed from Golding's translation of
Cæsar's Commentaries (1565): 'Of all the inhabitants
of this isle the civilest are the Kentishfolke.' Marlowe,
a Kentishman, may have introduced the quotation.
The less complimentary appraisal in line 61, ' 'tis *bona
terra, mala gens*' (good land, bad people), is supplied
by the reviser, who adds the words, *mala gens.*

IV. viii. 1. *Up Fish Street! down St. Magnus'
corner!* Places on the northern, or London, side of
London Bridge. St. Magnus' Church was at the foot
of the bridge, and Fish Street ran up from the bridge
towards Eastcheap (where Shakespeare's Boar's
Head Tavern was situated). This scene evidently
takes place on the Southwark side of the river.

IV. viii. 26. *at the White Hart in Southwark.*
Next to the Tabard Inn, which stood near, the White
Hart was the best inn in Southwark. Holinshed re-
cords that Cade lodged at the White Hart.

IV. viii. 44-46. *Were 't not a shame that, whilst
you live at jar, The fearful French, whom you late
vanquished, Should make a start o'er seas and vanquish
you?* Probably an anachronistic allusion to French
raids upon the English coast in 1457 (seven years after
Cade's rebellion), when Sandwich was captured and
sacked and Fowey in Cornwall burned.

IV. x. 31. *I'll make thee eat iron like an ostrich.*

That ostriches could eat nails and other iron was one
of the 'vulgar errors' common in Shakespeare's time.

IV. x. 56. *As for words, whose greatness answer.*
words. So much for words, whose pomposity corre-
sponds to the pompousness of yours. The line is un-
satisfactory and probably corrupt.

V. i. 5. *Ah sancta majestas, who would not buy*
thee dear? A six-foot line, frequently employed by
Marlowe for emphasis. It is found in the *Contention*
version.

V. i. 15. *Humphrey of Buckingham.* Buckingham
was brother-in-law of Salisbury and uncle of Warwick. Though a supporter of King Henry, he was
friendly with the Yorkists, and was employed on the
morning of the first battle of St. Albans (May 22.
1455) as an intermediary between the two forces.
York's armed return from Ireland and protest against
Somerset occurred in 1452. The incidents of over
three years of difficult negotiation are condensed in
the present scene.

V. i. 26, 27. *And now, like Ajax Telamonius, On*
sheep or oxen could I spend my fury. An allusion
(not in the *Contention*) to the madness of Ajax, when
he slew a flock of sheep in his rage that the arms of
Achilles had been adjudged to Ulysses rather than
himself. Shakespeare refers to the myth again in
Love's Labour's Lost, IV. iii. 6, 7: 'By the Lord, this
love is as mad as Ajax: it kills sheep.'

V. i. 46. *Saint George's Field.* A large open drill
ground between Southwark and Lambeth, south of
the Thames.

V. i. 100, 101. *Whose smile and frown, like to*
Achilles' spear, Is able with the change to kill and
cure. Telephus, who had been wounded by Achilles'
spear, could not be cured till the rust of the same
weapon was applied to his wound. This classical
figure also is missing in the *Contention* version.

V. i. 117. *O blood-bespotted Neapolitan.* Alluding to Margaret's father's title of King of the two Sicilies (Sicily and Naples). There may be an implied reference to the famous Sicilian Vespers massacre of 1282.

V. i. 140. *And if words will not, then our weapons shall.* The speaker, Richard, was two and a half years old when the first battle of St. Albans was fought.

V. i. 144. *Call hither to the stake my two brave bears.* A metaphor from the popular sport of bear-baiting, at which bears were fastened to stakes and attacked by dogs. Warwick and Salisbury are termed bears because of the badge of the 'bear and ragged staff.' Cf. next note.

V. i. 202, 203. *Now, by my father's badge, old Nevil's crest, The rampant bear chain'd to the ragged staff.* The heraldry here is erroneous. Warwick's famous badge of the bear and ragged staff was not derived from his father, but inherited, like his earldom, from the Beauchamp family to which his wife belonged. The Nevil crest was a bull.

V. ii. 58, 59. *Into as many gobbets will I cut it As wild Medea young Absyrtus did.* Not found in the *Contention.* The story is told in Ovid's *Tristia.* Medea, pursued by her father as she accompanied Jason from Colchos with the golden fleece, delayed the pursuers by slaying her brother Absyrtus and throwing his dismembered limbs into the sea.

V. ii. 78, 79. *If you be ta'en, we then should see the bottom Of all our fortunes.* The king was wounded with an arrow in the battle and fell into the hands of the Yorkists, from whom he suffered no further injury.

V. iii. 26. *Let us pursue him ere the writs go forth.* Lords were summoned to parliament by special writ issued in the name of the king. The parliament referred to was not summoned till several years after the battle.

APPENDIX A

SOURCES OF THE PLAY

The only real source of the Second Part of *King Henry VI* is the earlier play, *The First Part of the Contention betwixt the two famous Houses of York and Lancaster,* of which imperfect and slightly varying printed editions appeared in 1594, 1600, and 1619. The reviser, Shakespeare, worked with a manuscript text probably superior in a number of passages to that produced by the printers of 1594.

The First Part of the Contention is itself based upon the story of the chroniclers Halle and Holinshed, whose narratives are here so nearly identical that it is hardly important to determine which was employed by the original dramatist.[1] For the episode of Gloucester and the impostor Simpcox a dialogue of Sir Thomas More (1530) may have been used; the story was repeated by the chronicler Grafton (1568) and the martyrologist Foxe (1576), but is not found in Halle or Holinshed.

In revising the play Shakespeare's method was exceedingly painstaking. The 1594 version of the *Contention* contains only about 1250 metrical lines,[2] which in *2 Henry VI* are supplemented by some 2000 lines of new or largely revised material. But there seems to be no evidence that the reviser made use of new source matter. He merely elaborated out of his own fancy scenes and speeches with which the basic play presented him. He added no new character or im-

---

[1] Cf. W. G. Boswell-Stone, *Shakespeare's Holinshed,* pp. xi, xii, where passages apparently derived from Holinshed rather than Halle are cited. Compare, on the other hand, the note on II. iii. 13 in this edition, which points to Halle rather than Holinshed as authority.

[2] Eked out by about 700 lines of prose or corrupted verse.

portant dramatic incident, and can hardly be shown to have made any first-hand study of the historical sources.

Thus the consideration of Shakespeare's additions does not really involve a study of the sources of the play (apart from the *Contention*); it involves almost solely the question of the spirit in which Shakespeare improvised new speeches to fit the scenario furnished by the old play. This matter will be discussed in Appendix C.

The simpler and generally clearer tone of the *Contention* is well illustrated in the scenes depicting Suffolk's death and that of Cade. The 147 lines of *2 Henry VI* IV. i are expanded from the following 78 lines of the *Contention*.

'Alarmes within, and the chambers be discharged, like as it were a fight at sea. And then enter the Captaine of the ship and the Maister, and the Maisters Mate, & the Duke of Suffolke disguised, and others with him, and Water Whickmore.

> *Cap.* Bring forward these prisoners that scorn'd to
>   yeeld,
> Vnlade their goods with speed and sincke their ship,
> Here Maister, this prisoner I giue to you.
> This other, the Maisters Mate shall haue,
> And Water Whickmore thou shalt haue this man,
> And let them paie their ransomes ere they passe.

> *Suffolke.* Water!   He starteth.

> *Water.* How now, what doest feare me?
> Thou shalt haue better cause anon.

> *Suf.* It is thy name affrights me, not thy selfe.
> I do remember well, a cunning Wyssard told me,
> That by Water I should die:
> Yet let not that make thee bloudie minded.
> Thy name being rightly sounded,
> Is Gualter, not Water.

> *VVater.* Gualter or Water, als one to me,

I am the man must bring thee to thy death.

   Suf. I am a Gentleman looke on my Ring,
Ransome me at what thou wilt, it shalbe paid.

   VVater. I lost mine eye in boording of the ship,
And therefore ere I marchantlike sell blood for gold,
Then cast me headlong downe into the sea.

   2. Priso. But what shall our ransomes be?

   Mai. A hundreth pounds a piece, either paie that or
     die.

   2. Priso. Then saue our liues, it shall be paid.

   VVater. Come sirrha, thy life shall be the ransome
     I will haue.

   Suff. Staie villaine, thy prisoner is a Prince,
The Duke of Suffolke, William de la Poull.

   Cap. The Duke of Suffolke folded vp in rags.

   Suf. I sir, but these rags are no part of the Duke,
Ioue sometime went disguisde, and why not I?

   Cap. I but Ioue was neuer slaine as thou shalt be.

   Suf. Base Iadie groome, King Henries blood
The honourable blood of Lancaster,
Cannot be shead by such a lowly swaine,
I am sent Ambassador for the Queene to France,
I charge thee waffe me crosse the channell safe.

   Cap. Ile waffe thee to thy death, go Water take him
     hence,
And on our long boates side, chop off his head.

   Suf. Thou darste not for thine owne.

   Cap. Yes Poull.

   Suffolke. Poull.

   Cap. I Poull, puddle, kennell, sinke and durt,
Ile stop that yawning mouth of thine,
Those lips of thine that so oft haue kist the
Queene, shall sweepe the ground, and thou that
Smildste at good Duke Humphreys death,
Shalt liue no longer to infect the earth.

   Suffolke. This villain being but Captain of a Pin-
     nais,

Threatens more plagues then mightie Abradas,
The great Masadonian Pyrate,
Thy words addes fury and not remorse in me.
   Cap. I but my deeds shall staie thy fury soone.
   Suffolke. Hast not thou waited at my Trencher,
When we haue feasted with Queene Margret?
Hast not thou kist thy hand and held my stirrope?
And barehead plodded by my footecloth Mule,
And thought thee happie when I smilde on thee?
This hand hath writ in thy defence,
Then shall I charme thee, hold thy lauish toong.
   Cap. Away with him, Water, I say, and off with his
     hed.
   1. Priso. Good my Lord, intreat him mildly for your
     life.
   Suffolke. First let this necke stoupe to the axes
     edge,
Before this knee do bow to any,
Saue to the God of heauen and to my King:
Suffolkes imperiall toong cannot pleade
To such a Iadie groome.
   Water. Come, come, why do we let him speake,
I long to haue his head for raunsome of mine eye.
   Suffolk. A Swordar and bandeto slaue,
Murthered sweete Tully.
Brutus bastard-hand stabde Iulius Cæsar,
And Suffolke dies by Pyrates on the seas.
                 Exet Suffolke, and VVater.
   Cap. Off with his head, and send it to the Queene,
And ransomelesse this prisoner shall go free,
To see it safe deliuered vnto her.
Come lets goe.   *Exet omnes.*'

    The scene of Jack Cade's death, corresponding to
2 *Henry VI* IV. x, is in the *Contention* less than half
as long. It is almost altogether in prose, and quite
lacks the conceits and efforts at 'fine writing' which
the reviser affects.

'Enter *Iacke Cade* at one doore, and at the other,
maister *Alexander Eyden* and his men, and *Iack Cade*
lies downe picking of hearbes and eating them.

Eyden. Good Lord how pleasant is this country life,
This litle land my father left me here,
With my contented minde serues me as well,
As all the pleasures in the Court can yeeld,
Nor would I change this pleasure for the Court.

Cade. Sounes, heres the Lord of the soyle, Stand
villaine, thou wilt betraie mee to the King, and get a
thousand crownes for my head, but ere thou goest, ile
make thee eate yron like an Astridge, and swallow my
sword like a great pinne.

Eyden. Why sawcy companion, why should I betray
thee?
Ist not inough that thou hast broke my hedges,
And enterd into my ground without the leaue of me
the owner,
But thou wilt braue me too.

Cade. Braue thee and beard thee too, by the best
blood of the Realme, looke on me well, I haue eate no
meate this fiue dayes, yet and I do not leaue thee and
thy fiue men as dead as a doore nayle, I pray God I
may neuer eate grasse more.

Eyden. Nay, it neuer shall be saide whilst the world
doth stand, that Alexander Eyden an Esquire of Kent,
tooke oddes to combat with a famisht man, looke on
me, my limmes are equall vnto thine, and euery way as
big, then hand to hand, ile combat thee. Sirrha fetch
me weopons, and stand you all aside.

Cade. Now sword, if thou doest not hew this burly-
bond churle into chines of beefe, I beseech God thou
maist fal into some smiths hand, and be turnd to hob-
nailes.

Eyden. Come on thy way.

(They fight, and *Cade* fals downe.

Cade. Oh villaine, thou hast slaine the floure of Kent

for chiualrie, but it is famine & not thee that has done
it, for come ten thousand diuels, and giue me but the
ten meales that I wanted this fiue daies, and ile fight
with you all, and so a poxe rot thee, for Iacke Cade
must die.   (He dies.

Eyden. Iack Cade, & was it that monstrous Rebell
which I haue slaine. Oh sword ile honour thee for this,
and in my chamber shalt thou hang as a monument to
after age, for this great seruice thou hast done to me.
Ile drag him hence, and with my sword cut off his head
and beare it to the King.   (*Exet.'*

APPENDIX B

The History of the Play

On March 12, 1593/4, a London publisher, Thomas
Millington, registered his copyright in 'a booke inti-
tuled, the firste parte of the Contention of the twoo
famous houses of York and Lancaster with the death
of the good Duke Humfrey, and the banishment and
Deathe of the Duke of Suffolk, and the tragicall ende
of the proud Cardinall of Winchester, with the notable
rebellion of Jack Cade and the Duke of Yorkes ffirste
clayme vnto the Crowne.' During the same year the
play was published by Millington with a similarly
descriptive title-page, of which a facsimile is given in
the frontispiece of the present volume. In this 1594
edition and in a reprint of it which appeared in 1600
no mention is made of the author's name or of the
company which produced the play.

In 1619 the *First Part of the Contention* was again
printed, now in combination with the early version of
3 Henry VI (The True Tragedy), under the title of
'The Whole Contention betweene the two Famous
Houses, Lancaster and Yorke. . . . Diuided into two

Parts: And newly corrected and enlarged. Written by *William Shakespeare, Gent.*' The corrections and enlargements here announced are relatively inessential, and the earlier part of the *Whole Contention* amounts to no more than a new edition of the Quarto of 1594, though the publisher's intention was evidently to imply that it contained the large additions by Shakespeare which actually first appeared in the text of *2 Henry VI* in the Shakespeare Folio of 1623.

The close plot relationship between the *First Part of the Contention* and the *True Tragedy* makes it fairly evident that the former play was produced, as we know the latter to have been, by the Earl of Pembroke's Company before that company disbanded in 1593. This troupe had recently acted Marlowe's *Edward II,* and, if the inferences of recent scholars are correct, was at the moment employing Shakespeare's services both as actor and as playwright. Professor J. Q. Adams suggests that Shakespeare's initial revision of the *First Part of the Contention* and of the *True Tragedy* was made (in 1592) in order to enable the Pembroke Company to present them in competition with the original version of *1 Henry VI* (by Peele?), which was at this time proving a great success at the rival theatre of Lord Strange's Men.[1]

We have little knowledge of the stage history of *2 Henry VI* between the time it was amplified out of the earlier *First Part of the Contention* and the Restoration era. The Epilogue to Shakespeare's *Henry V* (1599) indicates that the Henry VI plays had been popular:

> 'Henry the Sixth, in infant bands crown'd King
> Of France and England, did this king succeed;
> Whose state so many had the managing,

---

[1] Cf. J. Q. Adams, *A Life of William Shakespeare,* 1923, pp. 136, 137, and the edition of *1 Henry VI* in the present series, pp. 133, 151 ff.

That they lost France and made his England bleed:
Which oft our stage hath shown; and, for their sake,
In your fair minds let this acceptance take.'

Ben Jonson's Prologue to *Every Man in his Humour*
singles out the York and Lancaster plays (i.e. *2* and
3 Henry VI and *Richard III*) among 'the ill customs
of the age,' which purchase the delight of audiences by
unjustifiable dramatic methods. He rebukes the authors who

'with three rusty swords,
And help of some few foot and half-foot words,
Fight over York and Lancaster's long jars,
And in the tiring-house bring wounds to scars.'

Jonson's contemporary and rival, the artist-architect
Inigo Jones (1573-1652) has left a vigorous sketch
of Jack Cade in costume, which may point to some
otherwise unrecorded revival or adaptation of *2 Henry
VI* in the reign of James I or Charles I.[1]

A revision of *2 Henry VI* by the Restoration
dramatist, John Crowne, was produced at the Duke of
York's Theatre about 1681, and published in the same
year with the title: *Henry the Sixth; or, The Murder
of the Duke of Glocester*. This work begins with the
quarrel of Gloucester and Cardinal Beaufort over King
Henry's marriage, and, after presenting the death of
both Humphrey and Beaufort, closes with the an-
nouncement of Suffolk's death and the success of Cade's
revolt. The cast of characters is reduced to eleven, all
save the Sheriff of London persons of the highest rank.
Duke Humphrey was acted by Betterton and the
Duchess Eleanor by Mrs. Betterton. Though in
general Crowne follows the course of events in Shakespeare's play, as far as the middle of the fourth act, he
retains little of Shakespeare's wording[2] and quite alters

[1] This drawing is reproduced in the Shakespeare Society
volume, *Sketches from Inigo Jones, etc.*, 1848.

[2] Crowne's Epistle to Sir Charles Sedley says: 'I call'd it

the spirit of the piece, which he seeks to bring into line with the anti-papal feeling of the closing years of Charles II by representing his odious Cardinal as an example of the vices of the Roman clergy.[1]

A sequel[2] to the foregoing play was written by Crowne under the title of *The Miseries of Civil-War*. This is in the main an alteration of *3 Henry VI*, but the first act, as well as the opening pages of the second, deal with matter included in the Second Part, i.e. the progress and final suppression of Jack Cade's rebellion and the first battle of St. Albans.

On February 15, 1723, was acted at Drury Lane Ambrose Philips' play: *Humfrey Duke of Gloucester* (printed the same year). This is a tragedy in the French style, consisting of many brief conversational scenes, which change whenever a character enters or leaves the stage. Only nine dramatis personæ appear, besides an Officer of Justice and two Ruffians. The whole action 'passes within the King's Palace in Westminster,' and within twenty-four hours. Humphrey, York, Salisbury, and Warwick are represented as high-minded gentlemen without much discrimination of character, and the Duchess Eleanor is absurdly idealized, while Beaufort is made a conventional villain. The indebtedness to Shakespeare is much smaller than

in the Prologue Shakespeare's Play, though he has no Title to the 40th part of it. The Text I took out of his Second Part of Henry the Sixth, but as most Texts are serv'd, I left it as soon as I could.' A recent investigator (Gustav Krecke, *Die englischen Bühnenbearbeitungen von Shakespeare's 'King Henry the Sixth,'* Rostock, 1911) estimates that of 2864 lines in Crowne's play 215 are taken direct from Shakespeare.

[1] Langbaine, a contemporary, writing in 1691, says: 'This Play was oppos'd by the Popish Faction, who by their Power at Court got it supprest: however it was well receiv'd by the Rest of the Audience.'

[2] This, however, was printed in 1680, a year before the earliest edition of *The Murder of the Duke of Glocester*, and it may have been composed earlier.

even in Crowne's pieces, and is not unfairly indicated in Philips' Epistle to the Reader: 'They who have read Shakespear's Second Part of Henry VI. may, probably, recollect most of the Passages I have borrowed from Him, either Word for Word, or with some small Alteration. Nevertheless, that I may not be thought unwilling to Acknowledge my Obligation to so great a Poet, I desire my Readers will place to his Account One or Two Hints, and One intire Line in the 24th Page, where Eleanor's Penance is related: Four Lines in the 38th Page, where Beaufort speaks of Gloucester's Popularity: Three Parts in Four of the Description of the Duke's dead Body, in Page 71: And about Seventeen Lines in the last Scene; some of which are so very beautifull, that it may be questioned whether there be any Passages in Shakespear that deserve greater Commendation.'

None of the revisions just mentioned enjoyed a real popularity. The most notable revival of *2 Henry VI* in modern times was that produced by the great actor, Edmund Kean, at Drury Lane. According to Genest the first performance took place on December 22, 1817. The play was called *Richard, Duke of York; or, The Contention of York and Lancaster,* and was adapted from the Second Part of *Henry VI,* with smaller borrowings from the First and Third Parts, by J. H. Merivale, in such a way as to give prominence to the rôle of York, which was acted by Kean himself. Queen Margaret was played by Mrs. Glover and Jack Cade by the notable comedian Munden.[1]

In 1863 an adaptation of *2 Henry VI* under the title of *The Wars of the Roses* was played some thirty or forty times at the Surrey Theatre under the direction of the reviser, Mr. Anderson, who, with remarkable versatility, doubled the rôles of York and Cade.[2] In

[1] Cf. Charles Lamb: On the Acting of Munden, *Essays of Elia.*

[2] This version was never printed and is now lost. Mr.

1864 *2 Henry VI,* translated with considerable modifications into German, was produced at Weimar by Dingelstedt as one of the series of Shakespearean history plays (omitting *1 Henry VI*), which were performed in celebration of the poet's tercentenary.[1] A more recent revival was that of the F. R. Benson Company at the Shakespeare Memorial Festival, Stratford-on-Avon, 1906, when the entire group of history plays, from *Richard II* to *Richard III,* was presented on successive days, the production of *2 Henry VI* occurring on May 3.[2]

APPENDIX C

AUTHORSHIP OF THE PLAY

In the vexed problem of the authorship of the Second Part of *Henry VI* two separate questions are involved:

(a) Who wrote the subsidiary play of *The First Part of the Contention,* preserved for us in the edition of 1594 and the reissues of 1600 and 1619?

(b) By whom were the large and often redundant additions made which distinguish the 1623 text of *2 Henry VI* from the *First Part of the Contention?*

Anderson informed Mr. F. A. Marshall (*Henry Irving Shakespeare,* Introduction to *2 Henry VI*): 'Unfortunately the manuscript with all books and papers were destroyed when the theatre was burnt down in the year 1864.' Another manuscript condensation of the Three Parts of *Henry VI,* prepared by the actor, Charles Kemble, is printed by Mr. Marshall, *ibid.,* vol. ii, pp. 203-246.

[1] For a detailed account of these jubilee performances see L. Eckardt: *Shakespeare's englische Historien auf der Weimarer Bühne,* Shakespeare Jahrbuch i. 362-391.

[2] An account will be found in the London *Athenæum,* May 12, 1906.

These questions can be only briefly treated here.[1]
The First Part of the Contention is either a particularly rough and unfinished work, or it has been very
unfaithfully represented in the published versions.
It contains a little less than two thousand lines, of
which only about 1250 may be scanned as pentameter
verse. In such a case arguments based upon elaborate
stylistic analysis are more than usually dangerous.
That Marlowe, however, was largely responsible for
the play seems now to be the general belief. Evidence
of many kinds points to his authorship: (1) the powerful, if rude, singleness and consistency of plot conception; (2) the predominance of Marlovian types of
character, boisterous and self-assertive, like York,
Suffolk, Queen Margaret, the Duchess Eleanor, Cardinal Beaufort, Warwick, and Cade; (3) a remarkably
numerous and striking series of verbal parallels with
passages in Marlowe's accepted writings; (4) metrical
evidence, which shows the author of the uncorrupted
verse portions of the play to have had many of Marlowe's most characteristic peculiarities of poetic style.

The theory that the *Contention* contains, besides
Marlowe's work, scenes by other writers, such as
Greene, Peele, or Shakespeare himself, has given rise
to much discussion. Particularly in regard to the
partly humorous scenes in the fourth act, in which
Cade and his followers figure, there has been mani-
fested an unwillingness to credit Marlowe's authorship and a desire to recognize that of Shakespeare.[2]

[1] They are discussed more fully in a monograph on *The
Authorship of the Second and Third Parts of King Henry
VI*, Conn. Academy of Arts and Sciences, 1912.

[2] Cf. J. Q. Adams, *A Life of William Shakespeare*, p. 137:
'The plays (i.e. *The First Part of the Contention* and *True
Tragedy*) show unmistakable signs of Shakespeare's work-
manship.' *Ibid.*, p. 136, note 3: 'There is no ground for the
supposition that Greene had a share in these plays. . . .
On the other hand, it seems quite possible that George Peele
was associated with Marlowe in their composition.'

I see little prospect of reaching conclusive results or these points. The theory that the *Contention* was written by Marlowe at all, or by any other reputable writer of blank verse, is allowable only on the assumption that there has been much contamination of the extant texts; and the inequality of style is more safely attributed to theatrical manipulation or careless transcribing and printing than to a fundamental division of authorship. The Cade scenes, as they appear in the *Contention,* are not unworthy of the young Shakespeare, but they bear no indelible stamp of his hand, and the wisest attitude toward them is perhaps that agnostically expressed by Mr. F. A. Marshall (*Henry Irving Shakespeare*): 'If Shakespeare's claim to have been part author of *The Contention* and *The True Tragedy* rests chiefly on the humours of Jack Cade and his company of rebels, we may feel ourselves at perfect liberty to believe that he had no share in them whatever.'

(b) That other writers than Shakespeare assisted in the revision of *The First Part of the Contention* and *The True Tragedy* into the Second and Third Parts of *Henry VI* has been often suggested, most recently by Dr. Else von Schaubert, who argues in a very elaborate dissertation[1] that Michael Drayton was author of considerable portions of both the Second and Third Parts. For this view, as well as for that which would make Marlowe himself Shakespeare's assistant in the revision, I see no sufficient evidence.

Whether Shakespeare's revision, as printed in the Folio of 1623, represents the work as completed by him in 1592, or whether it is the result of a series of recastings, is hard to say. It is natural to assume that the text may have been subjected to some alteration as

[1] *Draytons Anteil an 'Heinrich VI,' 2. u. 3. Teil, Neue Anglistische Arbeiten,* 1920. (The author accepts the old theory that the *Contention* and *True Tragedy* are not earlier plays, but pirated versions of the Shakespearean plays.)

often as the plays were revived on Shakespeare's stage, but there seems no ground for supposing that any very essential changes were made after Shakespeare had attained full maturity as a writer. Stylistically the Shakespearean portions of *1 Henry VI* testify to a later date of composition than the Shakespearean portions of the Second and Third Parts.

The study of the rewritten or additional matter in *2 Henry VI* and *3 Henry VI*, which in the former play exceeds and in the latter amounts to about three-fourths of the total length of the basic play, offers one of the best opportunities to gauge the trend of Shakespeare's poetical abilities near the beginning of his career. As compared with the original author (Marlowe) it is evident that the reviser, Shakespeare, had broader sympathies. He is interested in a greater variety of types of human beings, and exerts himself to do justice to such good but weak personalities as King Henry and Gloucester, who in the original versions had been left shadowy and negative. These characters are greatly improved and much more fully developed in the revised plays. On the other hand, the reviser has evidently less maturity and finality in his view of life than the original author: he sentimentalizes and frequently blurs the outlines of the earlier plays, particularly in his handling of the harsh and limited, but clean-cut. evil figures depicted in the *Contention* and *True Tragedy*: York, Suffolk, Margaret, Beaufort, etc. Rhetorical declamation and prettinesses of figurative illustration tempt him to undramatic and frequently inconsistent additions, of which the effect is to lower the dramatic pitch of the scene.[1]

[1] A number of passages in which the Shakespearean version deviates significantly from the source play are referred to in the notes to this edition. See those on I. i. 144 f., 235 f.; I. iii. 18-22, 174 f.; II. ii. 39-42; II. iii. 7 f.; III. i. 9-12, 331 f., 356-359; III. ii. 26, 344 f.; IV. i. 1-7; V. ii. 58 f.

This tendency shows itself uncurbed in *2 Henry VI*
in the Third Part the poet gets it under better control.[1]

In metrical matters also the habit of the young
Shakespeare displays itself. He has revised the
scansion of the verses with almost meticulous con-
scientiousness and in doing so exhibits mannerisms
distinctly different from those of his original. He
inclines much more to the use of the feminine-ending
or eleven-syllable line than the author of the basic
plays, and tends to avoid the weak-ending (final
pyrrhic) line and the alexandrine.[2]

APPENDIX D

The Text of the Present Edition

The text of the present volume is, by permission of
the Oxford University Press, that of the Oxford
Shakespeare, edited by the late W. J. Craig. Craig's
text has been carefully collated with the Shakespeare
Folio of 1623, and the following deviations have been
introduced:

1. The stage directions of the Folio have been re-
stored. Necessary words and directions, omitted by
the Folio, are added within square brackets.

2. Punctuation and spelling have been normalized
to accord with modern English practice; e.g., yclad,
warlike, housekeeping, Saint Albans, villainies (instead
of y-clad, war-like, house-keeping, Saint Alban's, vil-
lanies). The words murder, murther, murderer, murtherer, burden, burthen, etc., have not been normalized,

---

[1] For detailed discussion see *Authorship of 2 and 3 Henry
VI* (Conn. Academy), pp. 194–211: 'Shakespeare's Revision
of Marlowe's Work.'

[2] *Ibid.*, pp. 177–183: 'Metrical Evidence.'

the actual form employed by the Folio being in each
case retained.

3. The following changes of text have been introduced, usually in accordance with Folio authority.
The readings of the present edition precede the colon,
while Craig's readings follow it.

I. i. 137	ye F: you
193	Hath F: Have
iii. 46	fashion in (Fashions in F): fashion of
54	a-tilt F: a tilt
153	needs F: can need
188	an F: a
iv. 9	of an F: of
35	fates await F: fate awaits
51	threatest where's F: threat'st where is
77	goes F: go
II. i. 15	he would F: he'd
42	and if F: an if
47	ye F: you
91	Simon (Symon F): Simpcox
107	Saint Albans (Saint Albones F): Saint Alban
172	under ground F: under-ground
iii. 30	realm F: helm
iv. 38	Trowest F: Trow'st
39	enjoys F: enjoy
III. i. 10	And F: An
98	Suffolk F: Suffolk's duke
117	dis-pursed F: disbursed
328	Bristow F: Bristol
342	an host F: a host
ii. 147	earthy F: earthly
286	far-unworthy F: far unworthy
318	Mine hair be fix'd an end F: My hair be fix'd on end
327	consort F: concert
392	cradle-babe F: cradle babe
403	corrosive F: corsive
IV. i. 22	Be F: Cannot be
48	sometime: sometimes
77	shalt: shall F
117	Pene (Pine F) gelidus . . . it is F: Gelidus . . . 'tis
ii. 115	a honest F: an honest

179	an eunuch F: a eunuch
vi. 11	ye F: you
vii. 52	in F: on
viii. 60	an hundred F: a hundred
x. 1	ambitions F: ambition
56	for words F: for more words
66	I'ld (I'de F): I'll
V. i. 21	Should F: Shouldst
113	of F: for
149, 210	bearard (Berard, Bearard F): bear-ward
ii. 3	alarum F: alarm

APPENDIX E

SUGGESTIONS FOR COLLATERAL READING

J. O. Halliwell: *The First Sketches of the Second and Third Parts of King Henry the Sixth* (i.e. *The First Part of the Contention* and *The True Tragedy*). London, Shakespeare Society, 1843.

A. W. Ward: *Introduction to Henry VI* in *Renaissance Shakespeare,* New York, 1907. (Reprinted in part in *Collected Papers of Sir Adolphus William Ward,* iii. 231-291, Cambridge, 1921.)

C. F. Tucker Brooke: *The Authorship of the Second and Third Parts of King Henry the Sixth.* New Haven, 1912.

K. H. Vickers: *Humphrey Duke of Gloucester.* London, 1907.

L. B. Radford: *Henry Beaufort, Bishop, Chancellor, Cardinal.* London, 1908.

Mabel E. Christie: *Henry the Sixth.* London, 1922.

H. S. Bennett: *The Pastons and their England. Studies in an Age of Transition.* Cambridge, 1922.

Alice D. Greenwood: *Selections from the Paston Letters.* London, 1920. (The standard complete edition of the Paston Letters is that of James Gairdner, new edition in four volumes, Edinburgh, 1910.)

Copiously annotated editions of the play have been
prepared by W. J. Rolfe (New York, 1882) and by
H. C. Hart (*Arden Shakespeare,* London, 1909). The
edition in the *Henry Irving Shakespeare,* prepared by
F. A. Marshall, also contains very full notes and a
valuable introduction. That in the *Bankside Shakespeare* (New York, 1892) is useful because it presents
on opposite pages the texts of *The Second Part of
Henry VI* and of *The First Part of the Contention.*

INDEX OF WORDS GLOSSED

(Figures in full-faced type refer to page-numbers)

madding: **63** (III. ii. 117)
mail'd: **42** (II. iv. 31)
maim: **38** (II. iii. 41)
main: **8** (I. i. 209)
mained: **86** (IV. ii. 176)
mandrake's groan: **70** (III. ii. 310)
manent: **4** (I. i. 75, S. d.)
many (noun): **30** (II. i. 114)
map: **52** (III. i. 203)
marry: **13** (I. ii. 88)
mates: **54** (III. i. 265)
me ('ethical'): **31** (II. i. 142)
mechanical: **21** (I. iii. 196)
Medea . . . Absyrtus: **115** (V. ii. 59)
medice, teipsum: **28** (II. i. 53)
Melford, commons of: **15** (I. iii. 24, 25)
mere: **68** (III. ii. 250)
message, of: **79** (IV. i. 113)
mickle: **111** (V. i. 174)
minister: **57** (III. i. 355)
mistrust: **53** (III. i. 242)
monuments: **71** (III. ii. 342)
Morisco: **58** (III. i. 365)
most master: **19** (I. iii. 149)
muse: **45** (III. i. 1)
mutual: **2** (I. i. 25)

naughty: **32** (II. i. 165)
Neapolitan: **109** (V. i. 117)
Nevils: **17** (I. iii. 76)
Nevils' parts: **9** (I. i. 241)
nominate: **31** (II. i. 129)
nor . . . nor: **116** (V. ii. 74)
nothing: **116** (V. ii. 65)
number, in the: **56** (III. i. 308)

o': **39** (II. iii. 54); **96** (IV. vii. 114)

obligations: **84** (IV. ii. 104)
obsequies: **64** (III. ii. 146)
of (in behalf of): **109** (V. i. 113)
office-badge: **11** (I. ii. 25)
omitting: **72** (III. ii. 382)
oppose yourselves: **111** (V. i. 156)
opposite: **68** (III. ii. 251)
opposites: **118** (V. iii. 22)
or: **7** (I. i. 179)
order: **63** (III. ii. 129)
over-joy: **2** (I. i. 31)
overweening: **51** (III. i. 159)

packing: **57** (III. i. 342); **63** (III. ii. 111)
paly: **64** (III. ii. 141)
part: **115** (V. ii. 35)
particular: **84** (IV. ii. 123)
particularities: **115** (V. ii. 44)
passengers: **50** (III. i. 129)
pennyworths: **9** (I. i. 223)
period: **50** (III. i. 149)
perish: **62** (III. ii. 100)
peroration: **5** (I. i. 106)
pinnace: **75** (IV. i. 9)
pitch: **26** (II. i. 6)
point: **26** (II. i. 5)
pointing-stock: **42** (II. iv. 46)
poise: **33** (II. i. 202)
policy: **4** (I. i. 85); **46** (III. i. 23)
porpentine: **58** (III. i. 363)
port: **76** (IV. i. 19)
posted over: **54** (III. i. 255)
practis'd: **32** (II. i. 169)
premised: **115** (V. ii. 41)
presence, these: **93** (IV. vii. 33)
present parts: **117** (V. ii. 87)
presently: **59** (III. ii. 18)
prevention: **43** (II. iv. 57)

DATE DUE

The Joint Free Public Library
of
Morristown and Morris Township
1 Miller Road
Morristown, New Jersey 07960

MORRIS AUTOMATED INFORMATION NETWORK

0 1022 0087148 5